WESTONBIRT
Association News
2017

~ Bono malum superate ~

Westonbirt Association News 2017

Copyright © Westonbirt Association 2017
All rights reserved

Published in paperback and ebook by Hawkesbury Press 2017
Hawkesbury Upton, Gloucestershire, UK GL9 1AS
www.hawkesburypress.com

For further information about the Westonbirt Association,
please contact
Westonbirt School
Tetbury, Gloucestershire, UK, GL8 8QG
www.westonbirt.org

No parts of this publication may be reproduced, stored in a retrieval system, or transmitted in any form or by any means, electronic, mechanical, photocopying, recording, or otherwise, without the prior written permission of the copyright holder.

ISBN 978-1-911223-17-7
Also available as an ebook

British Library Cataloguing in Publication Data
A CiP catalogue record for this book is available from the British Library

Contents

List of Officers	*1*
List of Vice-Presidents	*1*
List of Honorary Members	*2*
Editorial	*3*
President's Report	*5*
Headmistress's Report	*8*
Careers Events Supported by Association Members	*10*
Deaths Notified Since 2016	*12*
Obituaries:	
Mr Herbert Arthur (Nick) Nickols	*13*
Betty Bullock	*15*
Sections News	*16*
Staff Section	*17*
Sections 1-85 (in reverse order)	*23*
Invitation to Association Members	*152*
How to Contact the Westonbirt Association	*153*
How to Order Copies of the Westonbirt Association News	*153*
Westonbirt Association Memorial Bursary Fund	*154*

Westonbirt Association Officers 2017

EXECUTIVE COMMITTEE

President Ms Karen Olsen
Honorary Secretary & Vice Chair Mrs Leigh Ralphs
Honorary Treasurer Miss Louise Matley
News Finances and Distribution Mrs Jenny Webb
News Editor Mrs Debbie Young
Representative on the Governing Body
Mrs Karen Broomhead
Headmistress Mrs Natasha Dangerfield
Staff Representative Mrs Joy Bell

Co-opted Members
Mrs Serena Jones
Mrs Mary Phillips

Support Roles
Membership Assistant Mrs Jane Reid
PA to Headmistress Miss Alison Salih

GENERAL COMMITTEE

The Executive Committee and all the Section Representatives

2017 ANNUAL GENERAL MEETING

To be held at Westonbirt School on Association Day, Saturday 14th October 2017

VICE PRESIDENTS
Mrs P Faust
Dr A Grocock
Mrs M Henderson
Mrs G Hylson-Smith

HONORARY MEMBERS

Mr R Baggs
Miss V Byrom-Taylor
Miss D Challis
Mrs S Cole
Miss B D Cooper
Miss N O Davies
Mr P Dixon
Mrs D Elsdon
Mrs S English
Mrs L J Evans
Miss M Evett
Mrs M R Farley
Mrs J Hutchings
Mrs V A Innes
Mrs R J Kingston
Miss J Marr
Miss E M Miller
Miss P E Morris
Mrs H Nickols
Mrs H Owen
Mrs J Paginton
Miss O T Pasco
Mr D Philbey
Mrs M Phillips
Mrs H R Price
Mrs A M Reed
Mrs J Reid
Mrs A Rodber
Mrs D Thombs
Mrs C Tilley
Miss S Urquhart
Mrs M Walding
Miss K S Yates
Mrs D Young

Editorial

I've really enjoyed editing this year's news from Association members from all generations all around the world. It's been a privilege to feel that I've been in at the beginning of future news too, by attending the inaugural Leavers' Tea event, at which the Year 13s had great fun speculating what news they would be sharing with us in years to come. Interestingly, one of the leavers nominated to be "most likely to be prime minister" was also named in the poll for "most likely to be arrested" – so watch this space, and we'll tell you in a decade or two whether their predictions were accurate!

The growing involvement of the younger generation looks set to continue with the appointment of the first ever Head of Association as a post within the school's Study One prefect system. Georgina Billingham writes:

"My name is Georgina Billingham and I am the new Head of Association at Westonbirt School. Throughout the year I will ensure that any and all Association events are well thought out and are enjoyable for all involved. I hope to be able to present the school in a way that highlights the way it has changed, but also how it has stayed the same. As well as this, I would like to leave a legacy of what a good representative of the school should be, and I hope that I can achieve this throughout my time in Study One".

This appointment speaks volumes about the high regard that the school places on its links with the Association, and I'm sure we will all look forward to welcoming Georgina, and her successor each year, and getting to know them at our future events.

It is gratifying to see that this year we have had copious correspondence from some sections who had been relatively quiet of late. Though, as ever, many of the younger sections are too busy carving out their new lives and careers beyond Westonbirt to send much news, the advent of social media as a means of gathering news will make it easier for their Section Reps to pin them down when they are ready.

Of course, news isn't the only thing that old girls like to share whenever they get together online and in person. Most reunions held at school include a generous helping of reminiscence and nostalgia. We'd love to feature your memories in a new publication, a kind of supplement to this News magazine, to mark the Association's imminent ninetieth birthday, and if you have any fond recollections or anecdotes that you'd like us to include, please email them to me at **debbiehawkesbury@googlemail.com**.

Finally, huge thanks to former News Editor **Serena Jones** for rounding up Section Reps and chasing copy, and to both **Serena** and **Karen Olsen** for their help with proofreading. Grateful thanks also to the Executive Committee for their strategic input and practical support in keeping the magazine viable, to the benefit of Association members everywhere.

Thank you for sharing your news too, and I look forward to catching up with you again next year.

Debbie Young

President's Report

Welcome to the third edition of the new Association News which, thanks to our editor **Debbie Young**, is so excellently produced. Although the News can still be ordered from our Magazine Distribution Officer in the traditional way, copies can also now be ordered on line or as a download.

As well as keeping members in touch with each other, it is a marvellous archive of what has happened at Westonbirt and the Association over the years. I myself find it useful as an *aide memoire* of events and of members. The school too finds it a useful tool and copies are given to the Library, the Head and various staff.

Mrs Ann Dunn uses her copy to find speakers for her Inspiring Women career days. Once again this year, I sat in on a careers day where she invited members back: some still at university to share their first year's experiences, some who were running their own businesses, and those that had not followed the traditional university route but had done apprenticeships, or with a secretarial qualification, had worked their way into permanent positions through temporary work. It was all food for thought for girls who had not made up their minds on which route to take.

I am now in my fifth year as President of the Westonbirt Association, and I thought it was time to reflect on what we have achieved in the last few years, and where we are go over the next five years. One of my first jobs was to create a Five-Year Plan so we could look at what we wanted to do each year and tick off what we had completed. At each Executive meeting, we have tried to spend a bit of time looking at changes we wanted to make, an activity we wanted to take on, a topic that a member had raised with us. A wish list, if you like, but a useful reminder of what we need to achieve to move the Association forward.

We have managed to arrange more trips than we have ever done in the past: to Bowood House, the House of Lords and two visits to Highgrove House. With the school, we arranged two Carol Services in London which involved the school chamber choir to help swell the singing. However, that did create logistical and timetable problems to transport them to London at that time of year.

In May, this year, we held a Leavers' Tea Party, instead of the traditional lunch, and what a success! At the end of the day, with revision over, the girls were more relaxed, and we had tea, scones and a glass of Prosecco in the Library.

Debbie Young got everyone talking with a fun quiz, asking girls to vote for the "girl most likely to... become prime minister" and so on. She read out everyone's choices afterwards amongst great hilarity. We were able to move around and talk to more girls, and **Charlotte Price**, the new Section Rep from last year, came down to chat to the girls too, having left nearly a year ago.

These events take time to organise, and our Committee are all volunteers. In this respect, we thank the school for their help in making arrangements and allowing us to use Westonbirt as a stopping-off point when we have local events. On our own Executive Committee we are always looking for help. Many of you have something you could give back, if only for a year or two, to help with a project. If any Section Representatives would like to join our committee and share their ideas with us, or even have a member in their year group that they know would be able to help, please consider it. New ideas and new blood are essential to keep us going.

We are particularly looking ahead to next year – 2018 will be the ninetieth Birthday of the school. Although our own birthday will not be for a couple more years, at this momentous time, it would be good to get together with the school to help celebrate the past ninety years at Westonbirt. We have been asked to join a sub-committee so that Association members can be involved in the organisation of events. It would be refreshing to have a volunteer or two from members rather than just our Committee to help plan our celebrations. If anyone has an interest in helping with the school's anniversary, please get in touch.

So, at both a school level and within the Association, we are looking for people to get involved. It could be for just a few months or it could be more long term. We would be happy with any contribution you could make. It all adds to the diversity that the Association has amongst its members. We hope that more people will consider coming on board.

We have already invited **Charlotte Price**, last year's new Section Representative, to join us to keep in touch with younger members. She is at Falmouth University. However, we are happy to use modern methods of communication and "Skype" her if she cannot travel to a meeting. The school has selected a new member from Study One, who will be seconded to our Committee to help arrange events for our Reunion Day in October. Not only will she be a help to us but she can also add committee work and volunteering to her CV.

We are also looking at ideas to bring Westonbirt to you and would encourage you to hold your own local events inviting people that live nearby, not necessarily from your own year group. **Serena Jones**, our previous Editor and now a co-opted member of our Executive Committee, recently held a sharing lunch in Bristol. Using our database details, she contacted sixty local members. Although some were not free to attend that particular event, they were keen to be contacted again for another. The lunch gave us the chance to chat with the members that came along about life at Westonbirt, which over the years does not change much. Certainly in discussing the food we could all have been there at the same time, yet one lady was there just after the war! Perhaps other members would consider hosting a local event. **Alison Salih**, at Westonbirt, would be happy to help you contact local members. Our Committee can also help with ideas or in organising a few copies of our latest magazine for non-subscribers to see.

I do hope you enjoy reading this magazine in whichever way you wish to do so. It is news from our members, collated by our Section Reps, that contributes to such an interesting record of life at school and amongst our members over the years.

Karen Olsen

Headmistress's Report

Another year, another group of leavers, and a year in which I believe we have received more visits to the school from 'Old Girls' and Association members than ever before! My thanks must go to the Association, and also to Alison Salih, my unstinting PA, to whom many of you talk to as you seek information, or indeed look to have a quick tour. There is no doubt that thanks to her efforts and those of the Executive, the Association is growing in size and activity.

School continues to enjoy a range of successes across our broad curriculum and indeed through the variety of activities we run. To say we punch above our weight is an understatement, and staff and students go above and beyond at every level. Year 13's university destinations have been varied, from the courses being chosen to their locations, and I am confident we span from Edinburgh to Falmouth with a number in between. The offers the girls have received are worthy of praise and their varied profiles are recognised in the grades required.

Recent leavers of 2016 (Section 85) have been keeping in touch and we have been delighted to hear how they have been doing, as well others who have been successfully completing their university courses in the last few years.

As the educational landscape changes, we have been keen to review the variety of qualifications this year, and, as we hear again and again, employers and indeed universities are keen to ensure that leavers are equipped with the right resources to rise to the challenge of their courses, or the demands of the workplace. BTECs will be running alongside A Levels. The impactful EPQ (Extended Project Qualification) allows all of the sixth form a chance to reflect on unexpected topics and to think about ways of approaching their work in an independent and mature manner; with applied maths skills, these make for perfect preparation for research skills required for university. This August will see the first of the new numerical grades for maths GCSE.

A number of new initiatives will develop further interest and feed the curious nature of the girls, and to expose them to a range of careers and routes for study.

The Inspiring Women's Day, Aspiring Futures, the Evening and Sixth Form Lecture programmes all create a gateway for bringing career and education pathways to life as speakers present a host of ideas. Many of these events are led by supportive ex-students.

Scheduled for next year are workshops with Amazon, Dyson and the Harwell Space Cluster, plus a host of interesting speakers. **Hermione Harbutt (Berry)** (Section 70) is one of our newly-appointed Westonbirt Champions for Inspiring Women, and she, with two others, has promised to work with us on a year's project, offering all of our girls an insight into her world of work and some an opportunity to experience it.

Hard work and persistence are two terms I think we espouse in a range of areas, and combining academic work with extra-curricular opportunity is always rewarding. The Sports Department is proud of all the girls' achievements. Currently, we have three girls trialling for the junior England squad and **Emily Brooks (Section 85)** in the development squad. We have a number of girls riding at a high level, a couple of outstanding athletes, and, given the number of girls we have, a fierce reputation for healthy competitiveness in all we do.

Commitment and dedication have also been great values in drama this year, and, under new directorship, the girls have been challenged to rise to meet new expectations. We have enjoyed three very strong productions in *Ghostly Tales*, *The Lion, the Witch and the Wardrobe* and *The Beauty of Courage*. This was a devised piece for the A Level group, which not only scored at nearly full marks all round, but was also performed as a fundraiser for the very excellent Nelson's Trust charity group. Our speech and drama entries have again been judged at a high level, and the variety of talent we have is testament to passion from staff which is cascaded to the students.

High quality has been an expectation of the music department, and we have not been disappointed. A record percentage of students have taken up instrumental lessons this year, and the concert band continues to impress. The string group has made significant progress, and we will continue to build on this next year. We have had some superb results from various music exams this year, and perhaps most notable has been Jemima Price, who, as a Year 8 student, has achieved her Grade 8 violin, dropping only two marks in her exam. Chamber choir has a reputation which now precedes them, and, consequently, they have performed in a number of venues. Christmas is a particularly busy time, and this year, I have to say I was proudest when sat quietly in Malmesbury Abbey as they participated in a concert with the Abbey Choir. I will once again look forward to welcoming back any of our Association members or other Old Girls, and I hope, as the school looks to celebrate its ninetieth birthday in May, alongside the hundred and fiftieth anniversary of Westonbirt House, that many of you will look to join us in doing so. May 11th, 2018 – save that date!

Mrs Natasha Dangerfield

Careers Events Supported by Association Members

Inspiring Women, Critical Thinking and Routes Ahead is the title of the event held at Westonbirt School on Friday 20 January 2017.

The day started with Year 12 attending a seminar and workshop on critical thinking run by Sheffield University. Following on from lunch, the sixth form were given 'treats', in fact, SIX from six former pupils discussing their varied pathways since leaving Westonbirt.

Each of them had interesting and valuable points to make, from **Sophie Ashe** (2016) with wonderful and amusing tales about how to manage a university freshers' week, to **Marina Souter** (1997) who, having begun her post-school life by completing a theatre design foundation course at St Martins, went on to gain a BA in history of art at the Courtauld Institute. We then heard how hard work, determination and persistence paid off resulting in her recently setting up her own company, Bonbon Design, London, specialising in all aspects of event planning. An extremely successful business woman.

Two leavers from 2004, **Suzie Drewett** and **Charley Edgley-Pyshorn**, provided further insights, Suzie as a highly-qualified property manager and Charley as a top UK and international HR manager. Both had seen tough times due to the recession, but had come through fighting and are now very successful in their chosen fields.

"The job may not be ideal to begin with, but take the job and learn something."

"All opportunities provide useful experience and don't give up if things get difficult."

These are just a selection of their pearls of wisdom!

Georgina McCulloch (2011) left school to attend Oxford Media and Business School and is now a PA with Hymans Robertson LLP, an investment company. It was a tremendous thrill to see what a confident and self-assured young woman she had developed into. After one particularly challenging job she told us: "If I can do that, then I can do anything! "

Fiona Vincent (2013) is a fourth-year medical student at Southampton University and on placement in regional hospitals. She emphasised the importance of work experience. It was clear to see that this young lady was going far and already had been the Academic Student President of the Faculty of Medicine as well as the student lead for the Faculty of Medical Leadership and Management. Fiona ended her talk by leaving us with three top tips – the Three Ps:

Purpose – have a smart goal: think ten years ahead
Proactive – seek new experiences and take up opportunities
Positive – believe in yourself

What an amazing group of women – we are so proud of you all. Thank you very much for giving up your time to pass on such sound and helpful advice.

Do please let me know if, since leaving school, you would like to share your experiences with current pupils and pass on helpful hints and tips about skills for life as well as career backgrounds. I am now looking for former pupils who would be willing to participate in the next Inspiring Women event on **Friday 19 January 2018**, and I can be contacted through the School on 01666 881332 and by email to adunn@westonbirt.org.

Mrs Ann Dunn

Deaths Notified Since 2016

Name	Section	Date of death
Betty Bullock	Staff	March 2017
Mrs Foden (Mrs M E Michael)	Staff	4/5/08
Herbert A Nickols	Staff	3/2/17
Lulie Webb	Staff	March 2017
Felicity (Lissa) Mills (Elliott)	contemporary of 39	20/1/17
Ingrid Divett (Jackson)	30	September 2016
Emily Bilmes (Rawlence)	27	30/3/17
Katharine (Katie) Clarke	non-member (sister in 23)	9/12/16
Sue Price (Judd)	22	19/2/16
Yvette Cregan (Birchall)	21	7/6/17
Esme Elizabeth Nicholson (Maitland)	17	28/1/17
Sheila Grove-White (Gandar-Dower)	12	11/1/17

Obituaries

Mr Herbert Arthur (Nick) Nickols
(17 January 1926 - 3 February 2017

Mr Nickols joined Westonbirt School as the school's first Headmaster in January 1981 and stayed until his retirement in 1986. Previously he had been at St Edmund's School for over thirty years first as Assistant Master, teaching Physics and Mathematics. He was later Housemaster, Head of Science and finally Deputy Headmaster before coming to Westonbirt.

He and his wife **Joyce**, became residents of Rose Cottage in Westonbirt Village, the home of many Heads over the years. He attended his first Association meeting in London in October 1981, when he invited past members to return to Westonbirt the following year to celebrate their Golden Jubilee. From then on and for many years, the Association alternated their October meetings bi-annually between London and the school.

By 1982 he was contending with the issue of girls wishing to move to mixed sixth forms, so he started some updates to Westonbirt to encourage them to stay on. Economics was introduced as a subject into the curriculum at A Level, and a new computer room was installed, incorporating the latest technology at the time. Common rooms were moved and modernised, new dining facilities were provided for staff and Sedgwick, and more study bedrooms for sixth form were created.

Mr Nickols also embarked on the appeal for a new school hall which involved converting the Orangery into an auditorium, with permanent stage and balcony, to use as a performing space and the venue for large meetings such as Speech Day. The Association President at the time, **June Wenban**, worked closely with Mr Nickols on the Appeals committee and, through the Association, raised funds for the oak doors and some of the seating. The first generation at Westonbirt School also raised money for a memorial window, designed by the old girl and artist, **Doritie Kettlewell**. This was originally destined for the then St Catherine's Church, however the Diocesan Advisory Council were not willing to accept any more stained glass windows. Mr Nickols stepped in and agreed to have it installed instead in the new school hall (the Orangery), where it can still be seen today.

Mr Nickols was a communicant member of the Church of England and upheld Christian values and regular worship at Westonbirt. June Wenban frequently stayed with him and his wife at Rose Cottage and often joined them for the early service at the church. In her tribute to Mr Nickols when he retired, June remembered on her visits that she could talk informally about the School and the Association. She also very much appreciated the Nickols' warm welcome and hospitality.

Both Mr Nickols and his wife took an interest in the old girls of Westonbirt and invited Association members to the school to talk about their careers and the Association itself. He encouraged several girls who were musicians to take part in the Music at Westonbirt programme. Mr Nickols was known to have a good memory for names and faces. An Association member from Section 58, who left in 1989, commented that he knew the names of everyone in the school.

In the summer of 1986 Mr Nickols retired, returning to Canterbury where he and his wife renewed their connections with Canterbury Cathedral and their local hospital charity trust.

On leaving, Mr Nickols became an Honorary Vice-President of the Association and kept in touch with the school and the Association's Staff Section over the years, occasionally visiting the school with his wife to attend functions, such as drama productions and Speech Days. He also attended the school's 60th Anniversary Service in Gloucester Cathedral. He last visited Westonbirt in the spring of 2010 in recognition of the school's 80th birthday two years earlier and the up-and-coming 80th celebrations of the Westonbirt Association in Summer 2010. On this visit he was able to meet the then Head **Mrs Mary Henderson**.

Karen Olsen

Postscript from Joy Bell, who represented the Association at Mr Nickols' funeral:

I was proud to represent the school and the Association at the funeral of Mr Nickols. His wife, Joyce, and children Kay, Chris and David, all made me feel very welcome and were touched that Westonbirt was represented at the service at Canterbury Cathedral. They all had fond memories of their time at Westonbirt. Kay recalled attending a school Sunday service with her baby daughter Rebecca, who drew all the attention away from the sermon! Rebecca was there today with her own baby daughter, and Thea nearly repeated the trick, until she was taken out of the church. As Mr Nickols was 91 years old, it was a celebration of his life and not really a mournful occasion. We plan to plant a tree in his memory at Westonbirt in a few months' time, and will be working with the family to plan this.

Mrs Betty Bullock
(died March 2017, aged 97)

I had almost forgotten how Betty Bullock was. How lovely for her to live so long and go on enjoying so many things, and then to die peacefully with family round her. We valued her very much in the French department, both as a most capable teacher and as such a rock-solid, kind, sensible and willing colleague, with a wide range of interests and a quiet sense of humour. She was the sort of person whose value is always appreciated but not easy to pin down in specific anecdotes.

Beryl Cooper

SECTION NEWS

Thank You to Section Representatives
The Association is enormously grateful for the hard work and attention to detail shown each year by the Section Representatives, who volunteer to collect and collate the news from their former classmates. Modern technology makes this much easier than years ago, with many of even the most senior members sending in their news by email. Some members have also found social media, particularly Facebook and Twitter, useful for newsgathering.

Thank You to Section Members
We are always pleased to hear members' news, so if you're a regular respondent, thank you very much for continuing to keep us posted.
 If you've not sent in your own news for a while, please don't hold back. Even if you feel you have nothing to report, we still like to know that you are alive and well, and that we have the right contact details for you. We also love hearing reminiscences about your own time at Westonbirt.

Youngest Sections First
We're continuing the practice of starting with news from the most recent leavers. In the early, heady days of their higher education and careers, reporting back to their *alma mater* may not be top of their list of priorities, so their news is often brief, but still interesting to read.
 There seems to be a correlation between the length of absence from Westonbirt and the length of a member's news report, not least because many older members give a thorough round-up of their children, grandchildren and even great-grandchildren!
 In all sections, we have listed members in alphabetical order by their current surname, to make it easier to find your friends.
 If reading any of their news makes you hanker after a nostalgic trip back to Westonbirt, we'd love to see you at our next Association Day (Saturday 14th October 2017), and the school also welcomes visits by appointment all year round. To arrange to visit, or for any information regarding the Association, such as the current contact details for your Section Rep, please do not hesitate to contact Miss Alison Salih, PA to the Headmistress, via her school email address, asalih@westonbirt.org, or by telephoning her on 01666 880333.

Staff Section
Section Representative:
Mrs Joy Bell

Mrs Joy Bell Hello again, everyone. I am still going strong at Westonbirt and love hearing your news - I have very little of my own to report to you, but I am about to complete my thirtieth year at Westonbirt. I can't quite believe it - I had to sit down with a pen and paper to work it out and check it! And I guess, in light of that fact, it was bound to happen that at the most recent open morning in March, we were visited by not one but two former pupils who were considering sending their daughters to Westonbirt, so I may end up teaching two generations of the same family.

Miss Valerie Byrom-Taylor Valerie promised more news this year and it is lovely to hear about her special birthday celebrations – congratulations Valerie!

In March **Deirdre Ward** very kindly invited me to lunch with a group of Holford girls. I was delighted to meet **Sally Clifford**, **Diana Gantlett**, **Lorraine Gibbs**, **Clare Gore-Langton**, **Carol Kynnersley**, **Gillian Ward** and **Davina Vetch**. Much reminiscing, and a special pleasure for us to see Diana who was over from Australia.

The year continued in a joyous way with several events in the summer for my eightieth birthday. I had lunch and supper parties at home for different groups of friends and even went back to St James's, Malvern where I was before coming to Westonbirt. It is now a conference centre offering accommodation, so a large group of us had a wonderful reunion there.

Miss Diana Challis I am still as busy as ever in Tetbury with duties as churchwarden. I volunteer regularly at the Arboretum, signing up new members, issuing motorised scooters and answering numerous questions. The new Tree Walkway, opened last year, is a great attraction. Do visit if you haven't already. I frequently visit my cottage in Yorkshire and enjoy the fresh air of the Moors, and when the opportunity arises I travel further afield. I am still on the inspections team for the Cambridge Board examinations, which is becoming ever more demanding. I frequently visit the school and lead historic tours of the house when required. I might say 'never a dull moment'!

Mrs Susan Cole I continue to enjoy my retirement in Tetbury, and am still as active as ever, playing golf, doing voluntary work, going to the theatre and cinema. I've again had plenty of holidays visiting Cornwall, Scotland,

Wales, Brittany, Tenerife and Dubai. The Brittany trip was for Westonbirt ladies to play golf, organised by **Mary Henderson**. We had a really good time.

In January I attended **Ann Dunn**'s Inspiring Women day at the school, and enjoyed meeting up with former pupils who were speakers there. It was lovely to catch up with them again.

My family are keeping well. My aunt will be 100 years old in July! My mother had a fall just after Christmas but fortunately didn't break anything. However, she lost the confidence to live on her own and has been in a care home for respite care since January. She has just decided to remain there permanently so we are now busy trying to sort out her house.

I enjoy meeting up with former colleagues – **Mary Henderson, Sheila Urquhart, Sarah Nannestad (Nutter), Gill Hylson-Smith, Jane Keay, Sue Montgomery, Diana Challis** and **Gill Fry**.

Miss Beryl Cooper Beryl keeps in touch with the Association, and I have been grateful to her on a number of occasions just recently sharing memories of staff who have died. It was lovely to hear personal memories of **Betty Bullock** of whom she also spoke very highly as a member of staff. Beryl is keeping well and sends her best wishes to all.

Mrs Dee Francis Loving retirement and getting the chance to take life at a more civilised pace. Reading, playing tennis, Pilates, dog walks, trips to museums, theatres and art galleries are very pleasant ways to spend a day. Holidays outside school terms are brilliant, too. Off to Norway in June and Italy in September - life is good! Long may it continue.

Mrs Mary Henderson We continue to appreciate the cultural, architectural and spiritual delights of life in Bath. I am now on the PCC of Bath Abbey, and this gives me a fascinating insight into the workings of a large and varied community. This year I am also 'teaching' the Easter Experience to groups of Year 5 children from local primary schools as they explore some of the stations of the cross in the abbey. Having finished my year as Lady Captain at Westonbirt, I have joined Bath Golf Club and am enjoying the challenge of an eighteen-hole course nearer to home. Tour guiding continues, and I take French school parties round Bath throughout the summer. In July I am shepherding a choir from Canada on their concert tour of Edinburgh, Durham, York, Stratford and Oxford. In May we are going with our choir, Paragon Singers, to Bath's French twin town, Aix-en-Provence, for the fortieth anniversary celebrations of the twinning and will be singing in a choral festival along with choirs from Aix's other twin towns: Granada, Pecs and Perugia. *Vive L'Europe!*

Mrs Jill Hutchings Highlights included a visit to the Hay Festival of Literature, where we enjoyed hearing several notable speakers, including Simon Sebag Montefiore talking about the Romanovs and Neil McGregor (recently retired from the British Museum) talking about Germany.

A Rhine river cruise in September proved to be full of interest, with very good company.

Our frequent visits to the Isle of Wight to visit our son and his family have now come to an end since they are imminently moving back to the mainland. We shall miss going to the island, even if our younger son does refer to it, rather rudely, as Alcatraz. (Since he works in London I feel he is biased). From time to time we take advantage of his flat there and venture into the busy world to see an exhibition or a show, but are generally very happy to see the M4 signs saying M4 West on the way home.

Our grandson is very happily installed in Leicester University reading politics (though where that is going to lead him goodness knows), and our granddaughter takes A Levels this year and wants to be an engineer. A school visit to Ghana triggered a desire to do this so that she could install water schemes in remote parts of Africa, but whether that will actually happen remains to be seen. I feel delightfully removed from the world of education which seems to have changed out of all recognition in the twenty-three years since I retired.

Mrs Gillian Hylson-Smith I am still alive and happy despite acquiring a troublesome back. I have been greatly helped by a growing ability in Pilates and a good chiropractor so life is looking up. The moral of this story is "beware of slipping in showers", but life is good nevertheless. I was sorry to hear of my predecessor's passing. He was extremely kind to me and punctilious in ensuring a smooth changeover. Joyce was extremely kind too.

Miss Margo Miller With the noise of bulldozers levelling the trees and fields below us, we left for the Bay of Plenty where we were remarkably lucky to find just what suited us both, Sue plus cat, moving to a house with an avocado orchard, while I was able to buy a freshly refurbished house in what must be one of the most beautiful retirement villages in New Zealand. It's on a narrow peninsular in Tauranga, with walks to the beach, and everywhere blossoming trees and gardens. Each house has its own garden which we can look after ourselves if we like, while hedge cutting and mowing is done by the staff of gardeners. At the village centre there are many opportunities to join in the social life and get to know people: this is an incredibly friendly community. When I had my ninetieth birthday, only a few months after arrival, I was bowled over by the greetings from people I hardly knew. What seemed like a sign that this place was meant for me was finding myself sitting next to someone from New Zealand schooldays - we were in the same form!

Mrs Sarah Nannestad (Nutter) Unusual not to receive news from Sarah, although I do know that she keeps in touch with school and a number of people through her golfing ventures.

Mrs Judy Paginton Judy has had a couple of health issues just recently but is on the mend and says that she and Stan are fine. Judy continues to organise walks with quite a number of staff and keeps people in touch through group emails. Well done, Judy, as I know that this is much appreciated by everyone.

Mrs Mary Phillips I am certainly enjoying retirement and being able to spend so much time with my five grandchildren. The most recent addition to the family, a little boy called Jude, arrived at the end of February. I spend time down in Chichester with one half of my family and continue to look after Emily and Harry at home for a couple of days each week too.

I still teach art to an adult group once a week which I find so rewarding without the pressure of examination results. This term I am planning an art trip for them (can't remember how many art trips I organised at Westonbirt).

I am also studying for another degree with the OU and have loved the opportunity to study such a variety of subjects. Plato is my challenge at the moment, and it is strange waiting for assignments to be marked rather than doing the marking myself.

Rob and I had a great trip to Venice recently for carnival and the opera. But Italy is taking a back seat this year as we have two trips to France planned. We love to go on walking breaks, and I am just getting ready for a trek around the Gower peninsula.

It was such a joy catching up with former pupils in January during the Inspiring Women event and I was amazed that **Marina Souter** had left Westonbirt twenty years ago. I keep in contact with a number of former staff, including, **Dee Francis, Sue Cole, Eleanor Kirby, Jill Green, Diane Browne** and of course **Philip Dixon**.

My thanks to staff who have responded to the news request for this year and a special thanks to **Joy Bell** who has taken over my role at school as the Staff Section Rep.

Mrs Helen Price We are happily settled in our new home and love living in the middle of Tetbury. I continue to enjoy my pursuits - singing, playing the bassoon, learning Spanish, playing tennis when the weather allows (not often at present!), and I'm still very involved in Sherston Church. I have retired from all my Guiding responsibilities, apart from being secretary of Ingleburn Trefoil Guild, and I'm coming to the end of my spell as chairman of Tetbury Footpaths Group, but I'm still chairman of Tetbury Theatre Group. I've stopped visiting HMP Bristol to teach dyslexic prisoners, but expect to be involved with Gloucestershire Youth Offending Service later in the year. We often watch live-stream performances of opera, ballet and plays with **Ann Dunn** and walk with Westonbirt friends occasionally. Trefoil Guild keeps me in contact with **Judy Paginton** and **Diana Challis**, and **Sue Cole** sings in the same choir and joins us for Tetbury Film Club. We also enjoy meeting up with ex-colleagues at the Westonbirt lectures and the meal after, and at other social occasions. Later this year, we're going on a cruise in Russia with **Jill Hutchings** and her husband, so the friendships we made at Westonbirt are still going strong.

Mrs Diana Thombs Book Club continues to flourish, with WB old girls, former parents and friends and I keep up with several former colleagues and old girls. Lunch in Malmesbury last month with **Clare Ryder-Richardson**, whose lovely mother had unhappily died near Christmas, and at **Diana Challis**'s home with **Dawn Elsdon** and **Jill Hutchings**. Also, of course, I meet **Helen Williams** regularly, my godson Edward being twenty-four now. Where does all the time go?

Miss Sheila Urquhart Apart from a few trips to Iceland, it has been a year for staycations, I was down staying in Tetbury with **Sue Cole** in October and managed to catch up with quite a few Westonbirt connections, even managed a trip in to school. It was looking in good shape, very impressed to see the bells outside Hades, to think they had been there all this time, and we were unaware of them. Holford was looking rather sad.
My other UK trips tended to revolve around golf which I am still enjoying. Sadly, I was not able to go to **Kate Fortune**'s wedding party, but I heard from Kate that it had been a lovely occasion.
If any of you end up doing North Coast 500 (look it up) do call in, I am just five miles off the official route.

Miss Sheila Yates Sheila still remains in touch with the Association but no news to report this time.

Mrs Debbie Young I continue to be kept busy with writing and all things bookish, which is fine by me.

I've just published the first in a planned series of light-hearted cosy mystery novels, *Best Murder in Show*, set in a fictitious Cotswold village not entirely unlike the one in which I've lived for the last twenty-six years. The cycle of seven books will run the course of the village year, and so far they're getting a great reception, both at my launch event at Waterstones' Tottenham Court Road branch and online.

I also held a local launch at the Hawkesbury Upton Literature Festival (www.hulitfest.com), which I founded three years ago. It's a free event celebrating books and reading, drawing an audience from far and wide to hear talks and readings by fifty authors, poets and other guest speakers. It was great to welcome **Bridget Bomford**, Westonbirt's librarian, as part of the audience, not least because I'd also recently enjoyed being a judge for the school's excellent Inter-house Reading competition.

As part of my work for the Alliance Independent Authors (ALLi), for which I'm Publications Manager, I also run writers' groups in Cheltenham and Bristol. I was delighted when former Westonbirt pupil **Corinna Turner**, now a successful published author, joined both ALLi and our Cheltenham group. I was very proud to introduce her as a writer whom I'd talent-spotted while she was a Westonbirt pupil!

All these activities have introduced me to a huge new circle of friends, but I still enjoy keeping up with many former colleagues from Westonbirt, including **Joy Bell**, **Bridget Bomford**, **Belinda Holley**, **Janice Malschuk**, **Mary Phillips** and **Charlotte Starkie**. I was surprised to spot **Philip Dixon** in the cast of an episode of *Sherlock*, playing a vicar (!), and looking as if he was enjoying every minute of it. Mary Phillips told me he got paid extra for being able to supply his own costume!

I continue to be an ambassador for the children's reading charity, Readathon, and have now trained as an official speaker for the Type 1 diabetes charity, JDRF (*www.jdrf.org.uk*).

In between all of this, I continue to go off in search of adventure in the family camper van, with my husband Gordon and daughter Laura, who has just turned 14. Last summer we got as far as John O'Groats and Orkney, which was fascinating on so many levels.

You can find out more about what I'm up to these days at my author website: *www.authordebbieyoung.com*.

NEWS FROM SECTION MEMBERS

Section 85 (2016)
Section Representative:
Charlotte Price

Sophia Ashe is loving life at the Royal Agriculture University, studying agriculture. She has joined many societies including shooting, engineering, food and wine appreciation society and polo. Sophia is looking forward to her second year in the fall.

Emily Brooks Since Leaving Westonbirt as Head Girl, Emily is now at Bristol University reading medicine, intending to specialise in surgery and possibly intercalating in anatomy or medical drawing. She has also made the lacrosse team, and is very much enjoying it.

Lily Cheeseman is at Oxford Media and Business school, where she is studying a year's PA Executive Diploma course.

Isabelle Corangi is at the Royal Agriculture University. She is having a wonderful time and is very much looking forward to continuing her studies.

Katherine Edwards From being Deputy Head girl, Katherine is now at Newcastle University studying geography. She is looking forward to her second year, and is keeping up with the lacrosse by joining the Newcastle lacrosse team.

Kate Egrova is studying at Durham University, reading accounting and finance. For her second year she is taking a placement year, which she is very excited about.

Sally Gibbs is now based at Royal Holloway University, studying English and American literature. She has been selected for the rowing teams, and is currently preparing for the BUCS regatta.

Maddie Hudson is loving Loughborough University where she is studying English and drama. She has joined the AU dance team, and will hopefully be coaching ballet next year. Alongside her studies she has been working as teaching assistant for classroom reading at primary school.

Scarlett Jones is studying a PA Executive Diploma at Oxford Media and Business School. She is still keeping up with the Wales Lacrosse and hopes to continue as she moves to London to find a permanent job.

Hannah McKenzie left Westonbirt and went home to America, where she is currently enrolled at Middlebury College. She is in the lacrosse team and loving the university experience.

Ellie Murphy is currently at Loughborough University studying geography. She has also made the second women's lacrosse team, and is having a wonderful time.

Ellie Parsonage is studying in Oxford at the Business and Media School with her Executive Diploma. Ellie has confirmed her place at Falmouth University for fashion design in the fall.

Nancy Peng is now at Oxford Brookes University studying accounting and finance, she is loving the course and the Oxford experience.

Freja Petrie is currently in London studying at the Royal Veterinary College reading animal behaviour and welfare. She has joined the rugby team and is hoping to get a summer research placement this year.

Charlotte Price I love life by the sea at Falmouth University. I am currently studying creative events management. I have also made student ambassador and student mentor. I have also joined the events society and Raise And Donate (RAD) society.

Francesca Quince is currently studying a PA Executive Diploma at Oxford Media and Business School. She is hoping to stay in Oxford next year to find a permanent job.

Hannah Reichwald left Westonbirt to go travelling around Asia. Since then she has been working in London and playing for Fulham Lacrosse. She has also confirmed her place at Falmouth University for the next year.

Trudi Seager Since leaving Westonbirt, Trudi has been at Sheffield University studying Spanish, Catalan, and music. She has joined the zumba and dance society and is potentially joining the gospel choir in her second year.

Jane Seymour is currently in Australia taking a gap year and working as a qualified ISA level 1 surf instructor. In September she will start at

Kingston University to study art and design history and practice, which she is looking forward to.

Hannah Southam is at Oxford Media and Business School studying the PA Executive Diploma course. She's loving the course and has also joined the food and wine society, having a lovely time. Once the course is finished she hopes to move to London in hope of finding a job.

Section 84 (2015)
Section Representative:
Stephanie Thorndyke

Subomi Ajibola At the University of Leicester, Subomi is about to complete her second year of a BA in Management. She is doing very well and is working as a part-time student ambassador for the University.

Yemi Greene is in her second year at Durham. She is keeping herself busy with studies and being the social secretary of the Durham University lacrosse team. She plans on going on her year abroad in June to Peru or Argentina to teach English for six months and then hopefully travelling further. **Yemi** is also going to spend six months in Paris afterwards. She sees **Immy McTear** and **Katherine Edwards (85)** regularly at nearby Newcastle.

Kelsey Heath Over in America, Kelsey is in her sophomore year (Year 2) of Ohio Wesleyan University and has declared her major and minor subjects to be psychology and history. She is currently working for a journal called *The Historian* in which she is the senior editorial assistant. **Kelsey** has stayed in contact with her close friends from Westonbirt, especially **Phoebe**, **Lucy** and **Mollie**, all of whom she visits when she comes to Britain.

Lidia Losada In Spain, Lidia is currently at University studying digital communication in English. She has recently come back from Cuba, is going to visit La Feria de Seville and is planning on volunteering at a camp, over the summer, in Greece. **Lidia** also regularly keeps in touch with **Evie Jones**.

Phoebe Lowes wrote to say that she is in her second year at RAU studying agriculture and farm management and enjoying it greatly. She is living off campus with **Rosie Nagle** and two others, with **Tilly White** living just round the corner. She stays in contact with **Kelsey Heath** who comes over regularly from the States. **Phoebe** also sees **Sophia Ashe (Section 85)** and **Isabelle Corangi (Section 85)** around campus and is looking forward to her final year at RAU, but not the exams.

Lucy Marsh At Cardiff University, Lucy is now half way through her music degree (BMus). This academic year she has been lucky enough to join the BBC National Chorus of Wales based in Cardiff and will hopefully be performing with them at the proms this summer. She is developing an interest in world music through singing with the University Gamelan Ensemble.

Elizabeth Motley is currently studying for a BA in practical filmmaking at the Met Film School, London. She took a gap year and did a three-month internship for a film company in Australia. Back in the UK, she worked for seven months with a catering company and served in the Royal Box during Gold Cup Week. **Elizabeth** managed to save enough money to go to Orlando and San Francisco with **Tomi** where they met up with **Louise Nicholls (83)** in Disneyland. At the same time, she acted as an extra for Netflix.

Rosie Nagle Over at RAU, Rosie is in her last year of her foundation archaeology course. She has also been accepted into Oxford Brookes to do an anthropology degree in September, which she is very excited about. Rosie is currently living in a student house with **Phoebe** and generally having a great time!

Stephanie Thorndyke I have had a very busy and unexpected year. I ended up cancelling my place at Oxford Brookes and decided to do things that I enjoy instead! I travelled to Hong Kong, Macau and Thailand over the summer, since then I have been working at a Sports Centre and playing lacrosse every week. I applied to join the Army, and then changed my mind and now I have just come back from Risoul, France where I worked a ski season. I have also just confirmed my place for work in the mountains this summer! I am taking every day as it comes and I'm really loving what I'm doing.

Daisy Truman has started studying midwifery at the University of Worcester, having taken an extra year at college to boost up her grades. She is loving it! She is very busy at the moment as she is in the middle of a long placement block, but almost about to finish her placement with the community midwives and go into the labour ward. University is great fun, and **Daisy** is sharing a flat in halls with five other student midwives. She has recently become an auntie, after her sister Alice welcomed her beautiful daughter Florence at the very beginning of February.

Charlotte Whitwham is mid-way through her second year at Plymouth University, studying physical geography. She has just finished choosing a dissertation topic and will be travelling to Southern Portugal to collect data this summer. Before that, she has a course trip to Ireland for two weeks to study the coastal area. In September, Charlotte will be starting her placement in Glasgow as she will be beginning her job with the Scottish Wildlife Trust.

Section 83 (2014)
Section Representative:
Amelie Sievers

Amy Chambers Not much to say, to be honest. I'm going to be graduating later in the year if all goes well and have really enjoyed my three years at uni. I'm going to South Africa to volunteer in the summer which is really exciting too!

Ruby Chan I am still studying architecture at the University of Manchester. The workload is huge, but I'm enjoying the course. I probably will keep doing architecture after my degree.

Bryony Curry I am currently on a placement year in an exercise physiology lab in Cardiff, looking into the cardiovascular responses of athletes to different stimuli. I will be returning to Cardiff Uni next year to complete my degree.

Eloise Fitzmaurice I am halfway through second year studying for a BA in geography at Durham University. I am still loving the course, and I am in the process of planning my dissertation, which is very exciting. Aside from work, I am still doing 400m athletics, and I am the charity rep for my college, so my exec and I have been organising various charity events throughout the year. I returned from my charity expedition to Peru in late September after spending five and a half weeks there, which was an incredible experience.

Jess Honer Finished my art foundation year with a first and am now in the first year of a fine art and photography degree which is going really well.

Staying in Bolton over summer, because I've got some marketing work experience in Manchester which I'm looking forward to. Other than that, nothing really exciting, apart from that we moved family home too.

Annie Ihonor I am still at the University for the Creative Arts, in the second year of a BA in fashion journalism, and I am currently interning with a company called Crew A La Mode and will most likely be going to Florence, Italy, for the summer.

Khadjah Ismail I am currently in my second year studying business and international relations at Aston University in Birmingham. Will be doing my masters in France or Switzerland immediately after my course.

Izzy Mathias I'm in my third year at Kingston studying film and creative writing which is going well. I'm also still working at the cinema full time, saving up to go travelling after I graduate.

Charlotte McCulloch I am finishing my degree at York this year which is very exciting. My course has taken up most of my time this year, so there wasn't much time for other things, but I helped with some of my friends' campaigns.

Emily McGuire Been a busy year! I left my job in London to go travelling around Australia, and I'm now back and living in Bristol working full time in student housing. I also run my own lifestyle blog and do freelance writing on the side.

Becky Murphy Been a hectic couple of weeks! I'm in my second year at uni on a social work degree in Oxford. I'm loving living here in Oxford, and I teach swimming part-time which is all fun and games too.

Mollie O'Neill I am currently working on a yacht as a chef and am really enjoying it. I've been doing it since last August and so far I've travelled to Croatia, Barcelona, Gibraltar, did the Atlantic crossing to the Caribbean, and now I'm in Puerto Rico!

Louise Nicholls I am in my final year studying human geography at Queen Mary's, which has mainly consisted of dissertation and exam preparation. However, I was also lucky enough to get a place on the field trip to Mumbai last December which was a great week.

Amelie Schiller I am currently in the midst of writing my dissertation on political theatre and have plans to work in a theatrical role in the future.

After graduation, I want to gain further experience in backstage responsibilities, whilst also working in order to earn funds to go travelling.

Amelie Sievers I am in my first year studying Psychology at Exeter and am absolutely loving it. The course is great, but it's been the things outside of it that have shaped my uni experience so far. I'm on the committee for our mental health society and have just been elected as vice-president for next year. I have also set up and am leading a weekly eating disorders support group and am in the middle of the handover of the uni's presentation support programme - all really exciting and so rewarding. I've also been involved in uni politics and have just been elected onto the Student Union's council. Overall, incredibly busy but all so worth it!

Kristina Smith Still studying international and European law at uni in Holland, have a couple of years left but planning an internship in Australia so that's exciting.

Alice Wordsworth I'm in my final term at Exeter, so sad to be leaving what have been the most fantastic three years, but also very ready for next chapter. I have got an assistant directing job over summer and am also going to the Edinburgh Fringe with my theatre company. I hope to be moving to London in September, either to do a masters in directing or to find other assistant directing roles.

Sophie Wu I am currently a third year student in the University of Manchester studying actuarial science and mathematics. I had already applied for a masters degree at several universities in London, hopefully I will go to London to study in September.

Sally Yau I'm currently in my third year studying pharmacy. Although it's tough, I am still managing alright and am hopefully getting through the remaining of the year and going on to do a masters this September.

Section 82 (2013)
Section Representative:
Abi Lowes

Hello everyone! Alice, congrats on your new addition I thought getting a puppy last year was responsibility!

Toni Arawole I'm in my fourth and final year of my languages and business management degree at UEA. It's been so much fun. I speak Portuguese now and am learning French. Hoping to do a masters in brand leadership next year. I also work for Apple, which is pretty amazing, and I want to open a restaurant at some point soon.

Saskia Burden I can finally say that after many, many years of hard work and determination, I am finally studying veterinary medicine at the University of Liverpool after graduating in Summer with a 2:1 in bioveterinary science. I feel ridiculously happy and have just spent two fantastic weeks lambing in Powys, Wales I'm incredibly excited to continue on the plan of becoming a farm animal vet. I also have plans to travel to and work in New Zealand to gain an insight into how sheep and dairy farming differs from here in the UK.

Lucy Fenn I'm living in Chelsea with **Fran Schiller** and I'm a paralegal business manager, so my day-to-day is gang stabbings and other stuff. When I'm not at my desk I'm often headstanding or doing something yogi because I love it. Lots of beautiful friends, travelling and spending time with my parents.

Alice Fyfe After graduating from Newcastle with a 2:1 in English lit, I've been working in London for a film production company called Rogan Productions helping to produce a documentary about Alzheimer's for Channel 4. Now that placement has finished I'm starting a new placement with a marketing company helping them make six short documentaries for SoundCloud about the music scene in uni cities.

Emma Gardner I am currently living in my own apartment in Bath, graduating in July with a BA in English literature with psychology. Plan on doing my masters in crime and gothic literature in September with prospects of a career in law post-grad.

Cassie Greenhill I've had a rather busy year after graduating in July. Currently doing a masters in sustainable agriculture and food security at RAU, so I've moved back home to good old Cirencester. Currently I'm also doing a three-month internship in London with the Institute of European Environmental Policy within their agriculture department. I hand my final thesis in at the end of September, and then I'm not too sure, just keeping my eye out for opportunities, but in no rush to sort my life out just yet.

Aisha Gross I am currently on placement year working in Kenya at Ol Malo Lodge helping out with the few tourists we have coming though and running the stable yard which I am loving. In September I am going back to Bournemouth Uni for my final year.

Hester Ingram I'm in the final year of studying business management at Uni of Surrey, graduating in the summer. I have a couple of job offers but just have to see which path I want to take, or maybe I'll have a break before I enter the world of work. It's all very exciting though, who knows where I'll be this time next year.

Annabel Jardine-Blake I'm just finishing up my fourth year at Cardiff Uni, and I'm moving in two months to London. I'm starting a masters at King's College in September in mental health studies, which is exciting.

Abigail Lowes I've moved to West Berkshire and work for the family business as a sales girl. I live with my boyfriend on the River Kennet and in June am taking on a fifty-mile charity bike ride around Edinburgh for charity with a friend.

Izzy Lysaght I'm enjoying London, and really enjoying my last couple of days left as an undergraduate whilst applying for jobs within the PR and marketing world. Before all that however I am travelling to the States and am going to tour the west coast with a friend.

Lydia Marshall I graduate from Birmingham this summer and am just planning on taking a year out to work before applying for my masters.

Georgie Mobbs After graduating from Bristol UWE in July with a first in business and management, I was offered a job at Wirth Research, an engineering consultancy. I have been working as project administrator in the operations team since September and hope to progress into project management in the future.

Lexi Noon After dotting round all over the place and changing uni and course, I am in my second year at Oxford Brookes studying business and marketing, currently achieving a first, and have a placement planned for this summer with a supplier for Estée Lauder, as I am hoping to go into marketing for a cosmetic company.

Laura Snape I graduated with a 2:1 in architecture from Cardiff last June, after the most intense year of my life. Following that I took a couple of months to recover and get back in touch of reality, got restless so did two months as a chalet host out in Meribel, and now I'm currently working as an architectural assistant near Bath. I'm planning to move in with my boyfriend after the summer, possibly abroad depending on job opportunities.

Alice Truman On 6th February this year I became a mother to our beautiful daughter Florence Alice Sharpe and engaged to marry my lovely fiancé Jack. I am currently on maternity leave from Westonbirt and I hope to return in December to continue my career in events management. Currently loving being a mummy and enjoying family life in Tetbury.

Fiona Vincent I'm now in my fourth year of medicine at Southampton University. Over the past year, I have been on medical and surgical placements across the Wessex region. I am the student lead for the Faculty of Medical Leadership and Management at Southampton, and I am going to Finland later this year to present at an international conference.

Issy Yerburgh I graduated with a BSc in physiology last summer and since have been on clinical placements in Bath and Weston. I'm looking forward to a summer placement in Malta studying diving medicine.

Section 81 (2012)

Section Representative:
Olivia Birkin-Hewitt

Olivia Birkin-Hewitt I graduated from the University of Surrey last year, and after considering different career paths I have decided to go into teaching, so from September of this year I will be training to be a secondary Spanish and French teacher. I keep in touch with some of the girls from Westonbirt and I still have a keen interest in lacrosse. I am currently the manager for the south west senior regional team, and I will be helping at the Women's World Cup in July.

Remi Greene Graduated from university last year and is planning on going travelling in May before starting a graduate job at KPMG in September.

Merii Kishi Graduated from university and is now working in a cake shop in Aoyama, Tokyo.

Esme Liegis-Canns is living in Oslo and still a full time legend!

Fran Schiller I have been living and working as a PA for a CEO in London for about three years now. I am loving it, although sometimes it's quite stressful. I keep in contact with some of the Westonbirt girls, mainly **Daisy, Harriet, Olivia** and **Megan**. Last year I lived with **Georgina Lee** from the year above and have recently been living with **Lucy Fenn**. My sister **Amelia**, after leaving York University, will be joining me in London next year. In news more shocking than the fall of the Berlin Wall, I was recently on a television show called *First Dates* which was an eye-opener, to say the least! My catch phrase on the show was "a man in tweed is all you need", which is perfect for an ex-Westonbirt girl!

Megan Woodley had a beautiful, healthy baby girl called Aurora at the beginning of April and both are doing really well.

Section 80 (2011)
Section Representative:
Emily Clare

Georgina McCulloch returned to Westonbirt in January to take part in the school's Inspiring Women Careers Day in January, speaking about her alternative route to a career without going to university.

Section 79 (2010)
Section Representative:
Sophie Martin

No news received this year.

Section 78 (2009)
Section Representative:
Amy Falkenburg

No news received this year.

Section 77 (2008)
Section Representative:
Portia Ingram

Sophia Barker Sophia is living in South West London and enjoyed living with **Sophie Milligan** last year. She's currently working as a school teacher in major prep school in south west London, teaching English, maths and humanities. She is a keen runner and running the Paris marathon in April, raising money for Mind. She's always hanging out with other girls from Section 77.

Emma Glynn After moving back to Gloucestershire over a year and a half ago, Emma has changed jobs but remains within the public sector of the Fire and Rescue Service. She has been PA to the Chief Fire Officer of Gloucestershire and Director of Operations for Gloucestershire County Council for six months now. It's been a whirlwind of change, but mostly enjoyable. She's living with her boyfriend, Ed, and both are enjoying their mutual hobby of modifying cars and experiencing car shows.

Portia Ingram Having made the exciting move to London in July 2015, Portia is currently working in advertising for OgilvyOne on the Southbank, and absolutely loving London. She's living in Wandsworth with **Bella Wisset-Warner** and regularly keeps in contact with lots of the Westonbirt girls. As Section Rep for her year, Portia (with help from other section members) is looking to organise a ten-year reunion next Spring, so keep a look out, girls!

Lucy Matthews (née Clare) Lucy is currently working as a 1:1 LSA at a primary school in Cardiff, and will start her primary PGCE at Cardiff Metropolitan University in September. Amelia is now four and Ben has just turned two. They're both growing up so fast – Lucy doesn't know where the time has gone!

Natasha Seel Tash is nearing the end of two years as a trainee solicitor at Watson Farley and Williams. She has spent eight months abroad in their Paris and Athens offices which has been a challenging but great experience. She is looking forward to qualifying as an associate in September and to hopefully join the energy and projects team where the work will largely be on renewable energy projects. She is still interested in aviation and is hoping to fly to France for the first time this summer with some friends from her flying club.

Lottie Sharland Lottie is living in London with her sister Clemmie and still counts the girls from Westonbirt as some of her best friends. She works freelance, consulting on and managing small businesses social media profiles. If you have a small business and would like any help with social media do get in touch with Lottie via lottie@lottiesharland.com.

Sophia So Sophia and her husband Tiemo Liu welcomed their baby boy Mason Pak Hon Liu on Friday 11 November, weighing 7.7 pounds. They are extremely proud and happy to be parents.

Section 76 (2007)
Section Representative:
New Representative needed
(Report from Jane Reid – Section 30)

Charlotte Burnham, **Clare Hooley** and **Joyce Lee** acknowledged the 2016 AGM notice. **Sallie Bale** acknowledged the 2017 Spring Newsletter.

Section 75 (2006)
Section Representative:
Charlotte Boyes

No news received this year.

Section 74 (2005)
Section Representative:
New Representative needed
(Report from Jane Reid - Section 30)

Lauren McEvatt has been in contact during the year.

Section 73 (2004)
Section Representative:
Emily Paul (Stephenson)

Suzie Drewett and **Charley Edgley-Pyshorn** were both guest speakers at the school's Inspiring Women Careers Day in January. Suzie is a highly-qualified property manager and Charley is a top UK and international HR manager. Both had seen tough times due to the recession, but had come through fighting and are now very successful in their chosen fields.

Section 72 (2003)
Section Representative:
Carey Milsom (Logan)

Carey Milsom (Logan) Got married to Stuart in September which was a fabulous day. Most of it went to plan. Church service near my parents and then afterwards at their farm which was lovely to be able to do. Still living in Malmesbury and working at the RUH Bath in cancer clinical trials. Enjoy seeing bits and pieces of what people are up to on Facebook.

Section 71 (2002)
Section Representative:
Joanna Colson

No news received this year

Section 70 (2001)

Section Representative:
Catharine Loveridge (Hallpike)

Amelia Annfield I am in London as a freelance art director, based in Hackney Downs Studios. 2016/17 has been a busy year working in London and Paris, designing a set for a Red Bull adventure show, doing art direction on several online and TV commercials and I have just finished a comedy called *Jack and Dean of All Trades* which is out on 16th March on fullscreen. I have just returned from a whirlwind tour of Kenya and South Africa which was awe inspiring and now I am back ready to take on more exciting projects. You can see more of my work and projects at www.ameliaannfield.co.uk.

Pippa Bremner (Goodwin Self) Living in Taplow, Buckinghamshire, teaching reception. Married last December, to a teacher, of course!

Jess Burger (Clifford) Imogen Nell arrived on 8th December and Jonty is a doting big brother to her. Other than that not much has changed. We have moved to Welwyn, near St Albans and are doing lots of work on the house and garden to make it fully accessible for Jonty.

Fiona Cameron I had a little girl called Amalie in December 2015 and moved from London to Edinburgh in August 2016. Managing to do some freelance work for Garrard and some other jewellery houses, also just finished illustrating my first children's book, which will be published later this year, and am getting married in the summer.

Rebecca Christopher (Landers) After seven years and one baby in Australia, Jon and I are moving back to England. We are lucky to be going travelling on our way back as a family through Asia, India, the Middle East and Europe (glutton for punishment with a one-year-old in tow). When we get back to the UK we will be searching for somewhere to put down some roots. Not sure where yet, but hoping to find somewhere nice to enjoy the English countryside.

Rose Farquhar Working on special projects at Nyetimber English Sparkling Wine, linking the marketing and sales teams and working on their international expansion starting with the United Arab Emirates end of March and then the USA in July. Still writing songs and singing with my band and doing gigs in the UK.

Natasha Finch (Rufus Isaacs) Natasha continues to run her fashion business Beulah London, through her store in Belgravia and online www.beulahlondon.com. Beulah is a luxury British brand with a vision to employ former trafficked victims in part of the production, giving them an alternative livelihood. Recently visited India where she did a fashion shoot and visited a couple of charity projects, she also is a mother to a beautiful baby girl Georgia Finch, aged two, and is currently seven months pregnant with her second child.

Hermione Harbutt (Berry) Richard and I welcomed our baby girl, Aurelia, in July. I am so enjoying being a new mum and absolutely loving life with her. The business weathered the storm of her arrival, and my maternity leave really well, and I am still busy bejewelling brides and clients from my two showrooms in London and Bristol. Darcey Bussell chose to wear one of my pieces for the *Strictly Come Dancing* programme on Christmas Day which was very exciting. I'm currently in the throes of designing a new headpiece collection, and Westonbirt has kindly agreed to be the location for the next photoshoot which will be lovely.

Ellie Harrington (Street) We are still in Tunbridge Wells and running a busy taxi service for two very sociable boys! In between rugby and cricket I am running a social media management company and a homewares company from home.

Tor Jones-Davies (Inskip) Bought a house with husband near Malmesbury(!), in eleventh year of working at Savills, director in residential development, running my own team. Well and happy.

Catharine Loveridge (Hallpike) 2016 was a busy year with moving to a little village in the Suffolk countryside and the arrival of Annie in November. I am currently on maternity leave, but plan on going back to teaching English part time at Orwell Park School in June.

Abby Moule (Warn) Things are good with me, our little boy and baby number three was born on October 12th at home and is called Atticus Elliott. The girls adore him and he completes our family. We are still in Chichester and are enjoying beach life. Not much else to report really! The girls are two and three now and all of them certainly keep me very busy!

Charlie Murray I'm a nanny looking after four children in Warwick Avenue, loving my job and living in Battersea so all is good!

Section 69 (2000)
Section Representative:
Lucy Croysdill (Fletcher)

Lucy Croysdill (Fletcher) Still living in Tunbridge Wells and working from home for a London company. Nina is now four years old and will be starting school this September. Looking forward to celebrating **Michelle Lawson**'s wedding in Malta this June with lots of the Westonbirt girls.

Lucinda Dungarvan (Davy) Continue to live and work in London. I have worked for the same Swiss family for eight years, the last four years have been based in the family office in Mayfair, my role is varied and very enjoyable. My husband and I have bought a house in Barons Court which is currently being renovated.

Clemmie Jacques I am currently sat on a beach in Sri Lanka finishing off writing my thesis. It is my most sincere hope that by the next year I will be able to tell you all that I am finally Dr Jacques! In my spare time I volunteer with recovering addicts and am an honorary research associate at the Charing Cross Gender Identity Clinic, with whom I'm also hoping to publish some journal articles this year.

Veronica Jones (Green) Still living in Buckinghamshire with husband, Tim, but currently also living the near full-time-back-late-commuter-lifestyle with my (nice) job in London at Bankside Gallery, next to Tate Modern. Miss the boys Henry (3) and Felix (1), (although not the mess and the tantrums!) so part-time hours will resume in a couple of months. Better balance!

Lucy Langford Russell I'm still living in Brisbane, Australia. For the past two and a half years I've been working for The University of Queensland Library, digitising the thesis collections and heritage items for our online repository, and learning support material. I'd imagine a library is one of the last places most people would expect me to end up working! Lots of high-tech optical/scanning technology involved which keeps it interesting, plus the opportunity to handle some fascinating heritage items from war diaries and political material to photo albums and architectural plans. Learning a lot! Not much else to report. Married but still use my maiden name out here.

Henny Vickery (Mercer) I married a sailor! We had the most wonderful winter wedding in December where **Sarah Clifford** drove me to the church, **Lucinda Dungarvan (Davy)** was the most efficient wedding helper, (I highly recommend her if you need a wedding planner!) and two of **Eila Greaves' (Denaro)** boys were my adorable page boys. Loving life living in South of France and working at the International School in Monaco.

Katie Wennink (Fortune) Have now officially become Mrs Winky! Or Mrs Wennink to the more formal types. We got married last June, having a very happy and intimate ceremony in Fulham Palace where a tree was planted for my mum, followed by a knees-up in late October down on the farm where lots of friends from Westonbirt came, so lovely! Still working as the dyslexia learning specialist at Thomas's Clapham in London. Oh, the irony! I love it and feel very grateful to be doing something so worthwhile. Otherwise, just normal life ticking along in sunny Costa del Brixton.

Section 68 (1999)

Section Representative:
New Representative needed (Report compiled by Jane Reid)

Nicky Blythe (Pike), **Samantha Scott (Symons)** and **Pippa Vowles** acknowledged the AGM notice.

Camilla Pole acknowledged the Spring 2017 Newsletter – she has a new email address.

An automatic response from **Charlie Wood** in August 2016 said that she was on maternity leave (as had the message in February 2016).

Section 67 (1998)
Section Representative:
Julia Collis (Bleasdale)

Leila Barton (Rawes) Since getting married in September 2015, lots has happened. Merrick and I have made the move from London to Oxfordshire and are loving the more chilled lifestyle of country living. We welcomed Jack Alexander at the beginning of October and absolutely adore being a family of three. My dream of being a mum finally fulfilled! My parents have moved back to the UK and are wonderfully settled in North Norfolk and it's been a happy adjustment having them just a few hours' drive away especially with their new status as grandparents. All in all, life is good!

Julia Collis (Bleasdale) We are in the process of moving house. We do this with a mix of sadness leaving a village which we love but excitement for the future. Over the last year, our daughter Isabel has started in the nursery at Westonbirt Prep and Tobias has moved into Year 1. They both love school and are very lucky to benefit from the wonderful grounds and facilities on offer. Family life keeps me both happy and busy!

Section 66 (1997)
Section Representative:
Katie Mason (Eves)

Polly Allen (Mann) Still working in TV documentary between London and Oxfordshire. Two of my three children at school now but still total chaos. My sister **Becky** is my new next-door neighbour which is lovely. Yet to persuade **Jemima** to join the commune - understandably she is too busy keeping away from us in New Zealand!

Louise Banerjee (Barnwell) Went back to work again in September after her second baby and is enjoying the calm before the storm of taking over a boarding house of sixty-four teenage girls at the start of the new academic year. I think we must be mad! Lyla, who will be starting school in September, is very excited. Hamish, who is now seventeen months, doesn't have a clue what is about to hit him! All is otherwise well and still enjoying the Northamptonshire countryside.

Zarina Chatwin (Marsh) is settling in to life in Singapore. Caspar (6) and Ottilia (4) are enjoying school and Atticus (3) soon to follow. Enjoying being stay-at-home mother.

Clare Conley (Rankin) Living in San Diego, California with husband Jack Conley and two children, Savannah (8) and Olivia (6). I work for Qualcomm, for whom I have worked, for five years in a marketing role - currently lead their corporate communications team. Having now logged nearly seventeen years in the US, I love my annual trips back to the UK, but sun and palm trees have won me over!

Sally Cullum (Hopewell) I was fully promoted last year to senior finance assistant for the Boughton Estates Ltd. I manager a team of three others and oversee the accounts for Boughton and Contour, a landscape project company. Work takes up a considerable amount of my time but we also bought a Victorian property last year that needs a fair bit of paint/roof and chimney repairs/re-pointing etc, so I go between paintbrush and spreadsheets at the minute.

Siobhan Dunn (Suffield Jones) Still enjoying my career break, with one year left to go. Feeling very privileged to be a stay-at-home mother to Lydia, aged six, and Jeremy, nearly four. I love spending time with them and also down at our allotment.

Nikki Earthrowl (Roberts) back at work post maternity leave. Toby is now a year old and a happy boy. Ben is nearly five and getting up to all sorts of mischief! I'm still working for Macquarie bank as an oil trader specialising in physical financing, I moved on from geology a while back, but am loving the change in direction and get my mountain fix from visiting my mum. Otherwise, living in Surrey and bravely battling the trains into town daily.

Jessica Green (White) we're loving living in Wiltshire. I'm currently on maternity leave from GP work having had Emmy last year. We're all completely smitten, and the twins love having a baby to 'look after'. Jake and Rosie have just turned four, so start school this year. I'm doing some teaching at Swindon Hospital one day a week, which is great, and will go back to GP work in September. Be great to catch up with everyone - it's crazy that it's been twenty years since we left.

Kate Mahoney Married and has a six-year-old daughter Poppy. Lives in Catford, London. Working as a freelance advertising agency producer making commercials.

Katie Mason (Eves) just finishing maternity leave. Rosa is now seven months and very smiley. Cecily is three and a very happy little soul! I'm still working for a small NGO working on malaria and Neglected Tropical Disease control in emergencies. Otherwise, living in the Cotswolds and currently camping in our neighbour's house while we try to buy it!

Jo Ogilvy (Llewelyn) now lives in Somerset and is enjoying being so close to the source of so much good cheese and cider. She has a little boy called Antony who is three. She still works for the same company as she has always done, which feels deeply unimaginative given she spends her whole time helping other people change jobs. If ever any one is heading to the West Country and wants a pit stop, then be in touch, as living so far away means this is often the best way of seeing people! Lots of love to all and cannot believe it's been twenty years since we left.

Sam Vermaak (Russell) I'm still TB vaccine programme manager at Oxford Uni's Jenner Institute, but I'm about to move over to another role setting up and managing an international research network, developing vaccines against TB, leishmaniasis, leprosy and burkholderia, which I'm really looking forward to - it should be a very interesting and challenging new job. On the home front, Corne and I successfully sold our first house project and have bought our second, so we are now based in Abingdon, spending all our time working on the new house and once again living in a building site!

Camilla Wilson is still enjoying living in London and running Redwing PR, a lifestyle public relations agency. Camilla is just back from visiting **Pea Lawson (Gordon Dean)** in Miami, where she had the most brilliant time soaking up the sun and fun and particularly hanging out with Pea's little boy, Ziggy, who is Camilla's adorable godson. As we reminisced, we found it hard to believe it is coming up to twenty years since we left Westonbirt.

Section 65 (1996)
Section Representative:
Catherine Hirons (Charlton)

Well, goodness me ladies – turning forty this year and twenty-one years since we left Westonbirt. So much has changed, but it is great that so many of you continue to contribute. It is so lovely to hear what everyone is up to with work, family and travel. Thinking always when we do this of **Cara** and **Louisa**. Hope you all have a great summer.

Sophie Bampton Business as usual for me. Loving being a mum. Beau is amazing. Walking and lots of baby chatter. I can't imagine running two companies with two children, but I guess people all over do it. I'll just have to be more organised. Baby brain never really left.

Alexandra Butler (Earley) Not much change here, loving life in Sherston and still working in Bristol. Both girls now at school, which means I'm working a few more hours. In need of some sunshine, so the annual Easter trip to Barcelona to visit the in-laws can't come quickly enough.

Rachel Carey (Kidd) I am loving life back in the UK after fourteen years in Australia and being so close to my family and my gorgeous nephews. I am living life between UK and France (Alps) at the moment. Sadly, my hubby and I have split up and he has moved back to the Sydney. All is amicable, and I am ready for my next adventure. I am living a nomadic lifestyle but use Mum's as a base in Staffordshire. If anyone knows of anyone who wants their chalet run and managed, please let me know if in the Three Valleys as looking for a position for next season. However need accommodation for myself and my eleven-year-old lab!

Fiona Christie (Thorne) Jon and I are about to put our house on the market but have yet to find the house to move to. An exciting, albeit a little daunting, year ahead! All three girls are doing very well. Still running my little art club at my daughter's school and finally finished my website (www.lulaandpops.com) for my pictures. Both keeping me busy!

Laura Cristau After a tough previous year, things are finally moving forwards very positively. The sale of the family home in the Cotswolds has nudged me to get my act together. I have been preparing a project with a group of like-minded friends and, a bit dauntingly, I have finally taken the step to leave the comfort of Paris (moving in August) and head for fresher pastures in the direction of the Loire region and its chateaux. We are setting up an eco/bio farm which will offer various activities and retreats. Am very excited about this prospect, as is my daughter, just turned seven, who is already imagining herself cavorting freely in fields and on horseback, and planning quite an extensive children's play space. It will make a radical change after having been in the capital for fifteen years, but if I don't do it now, I won't ever do it!

Am also very excited about seeing **Alex Early** in May and catching up after so long. Also very much looking forward to **Nat Simpson**'s wedding - so excited for her! Looking forward to reading your news and if ever anyone is heading my way, please don't hesitate to give me a shout, I would love to catch up.

Louisa Gallimore Audrey was born last June and is already keeping us on our toes. Sam is now four and he completely adores her, although there's not a mobile phone charger that hasn't been chewed, and taking her to the beach means constant checking she hasn't eaten a load of sand! We braved the twenty-four-hour journey back to Australia for Christmas, which was lovely, and are now just gearing up for another summer in France.

Laetitia Glossop My news was potentially changed somewhat yesterday with the general election announcement. I am hoping for a winnable seat but have no idea whether this will happen or what seats will be available. Hopefully I will find out fairly soon. Other than political activity, I moved jobs last year becoming a partner and head of asset management at Hammond Partners last September. Back with politics, I am chairing the party's technology forum's FinTech working group, which is very interesting. I had an article published in October on financial education on *Conservative Home* and am very involved in fundraising for marginal seats. So, a busy few weeks ahead, whether I stand or not!

Claire Hall (Lewis) Life is as hectic as ever in the Hall household. I'm still living in Crowthorne, Berkshire, with my hubby Chris and kids Ryan (13), Katie (12) and Harry (9). Starting to feel old with two kids in secondary school. Ryan has now chosen his GCSEs and is doing his bronze DofE. We managed our first 'big' family holiday last year (Mexico) which was amazing. Sadly we can't go every year, but the kids have now got the travel bug, so hopefully we will be managing a few more holidays. Can't believe we will be turning forty later this year! Hopefully we will be celebrating in style!

Emily Haslam (Marshall) Our new puppy arrived and she is heaven. Although she is super naughty and inquisitive - she has been here two weeks and fallen down a storm drain, got stuck in the railings and had to spend the night at the hospital as she ate some poisonous leaves! We are still trying to get planning to extend our home in Cornwall. It is just too tiny when it is invaded with all our family, so we would love to add on a kitchen and boot room, which is proving very difficult! Work is all good - exciting times with more crazy plans there. **Harriet** (my sister) is having her second bambino later this year which is very cool and still living in Gloucestershire which her whole team adore.

Lucy Heyworth (Pearson) We're trying to move house from London to Oxfordshire. Not being particularly lucky, a house we were trying to buy fell through and our buyers have just pulled out of the sale of our house. Fingers crossed this time next year we'll be somewhere new.

Caroline Kearsley (White) We are now off the boat and back in Falmouth. We had an amazing fourteen months away, sailing from the UK to Crete, but have settled happily back into Cornish life. Honey has started secondary school, and Amelie is back at our local primary school. (Both pleased that I am not trying to teach them any more.) We are unexpectedly expecting another baby in March which is a mini miracle, as I was told by doctors that it would never happen. We are so lucky and very happy.

Amy Keyter (Tucker-Brown) We are moving back to Cheltenham so kids can be nearer to grandparents and moving jobs after a busy ten years building the resort. Sad to leave Cornwall but looking forward to being close by to **Sophie** and others.

Isabel Langly-Smith (Lowndes) Supposedly this last year has been our year of simplicity, so we have sold out of life in London and finally bought a lovely home in Hampshire, all three kids are very settled here, and apart from running their lives, managing the house and writing the odd nutrition blog for my husband's business, I'm not really tied up in anything else. No longer having my own business is now a huge weight off my mind! Who knows what next year will bring? I think about Westonbirt life often, especially now my kids are growing up and 'serious' schooling is coming into our thoughts quite a lot.

Diana Lewis I qualified as a teacher last year, and am now working as a science teacher in West Sussex. I'm hoping I can get to teach some food tech next year! The holidays are great, but I am more than putting in the hours to justify the long holidays. I'm looking forward to a getaway at Easter and the early morning dog walks in the daylight. I am also still doing a bit of work as a driving instructor and running a Brownie group, so am certainly keeping busy at the moment!

Harriet Mackinlay (Bradley) We moved house in September (still in Tonbridge), but have not been very organised and are still living in a 1980s paradise (everything textured and either pink or royal blue). We are very happy with it though, and the cat approves, which is the main thing. Still working at the Home Office and have a great team there which makes all the difference. We've also embarked on IVF in a blatant attempt to have more interesting news for next year!

Hannah Pope (West) I finished work in December and I'm back to full time motherhood. I've done the inevitable and joined the school's PTA. Anyone seen *Bad Moms*?! My youngest will start preschool in September and I'm looking forward to getting more than five seconds to myself!

Natacha Prudhomme (Marangos) Still living in beautiful Burgundy with my two lovely girls, Léli-Louise, aged nine, and Adèle, aged six now. I'm still a foster parent which isn't easy every day but enjoying it loads. Really looking forward to going to **Nat**'s wedding in October this year.

Nathalie Simpson For me the last eighteen months since I came back from Hong Kong have been amazing. Warren and I got engaged in December so we're over the moon and starting slowly to plan our wedding. 2017 will be a very exciting year!

Una Strauss (Laffan) Living in Bayswater, London, with husband Jamie, and two little girls. Still working (less!) teaching yoga and often thinking of how to escape the English winters by going home to Mexico (Still!)

Jo Wilkie Well, a year on and I am still in the same job, though not sure I really see it as long term. I'm tempted to step away from financial services, but at the same time don't want to drop too far down the ladder by going into another industry. Decisions, decisions. I've gone from an American-owned company to South-African-owned and now Australian-owned, but no trips to Oz so far and nothing scheduled, though I have to say I rather like being at home!

No surprise that sport is still my big focus, and despite going into the European Age Group Duathlon Champs in far from great form last April, I surprised myself and came second in my age category. Very proud to stand up on the podium and receive my silver medal and thoroughly enjoyed the whole adventure. Heading to Spain for the event this year, but again am not as fit as I would like to be having split my knee open falling in a cross-country race at the beginning of the year. Had seven stitches, crutches and was out of action completely for five weeks. Work had to take place from the comfort of my sofa for a while as I was immobile. It's still healing, but fair to say I have some gory pictures and will have an impressive scar!

Had a great time in Lisbon for the European Tri champs last summer; saw the sights and tasted some amazing food and enjoyed post-race celebrations with **Alys Mathew**. Our sporting paths continue to cross. Looking forward to a family holiday in Cornwall over Easter and planning on meeting up with **Caroline Kearsley** and her family. It's been a few years, possibly four or five?!

Section 64 (1995)
Section Representative:
Emma Lloyd-Williams (Leek)

Alex Batho (Battle) I've finally quit working in London and in November I joined my parents publishing business, Countryside Books. I now walk to work in ten minutes instead of commuting for three hours a day which has been a brilliant decision. I'm really enjoying the new job and it's great seeing our two daughters a bit more. Life is pretty busy but good.

Emma Lloyd-Williams (Leek) Still living in Kingston with my partner Alec and daughter Mollie. I have decided to take a break from work whilst Mollie settles into school life. Keeping myself occupied with running the church fete and gardening.

Victoria Knight (Murray) We moved to a new house last October but are still in Nettlebed just outside of Henley. I'm married with two daughters aged seven and nine and I'm now back working full time at Savills.

Victoria Stevens (White) No major news from me, much the same as last time really. Still see **Zoe** and **Alice Gaskell (Woods)** regularly which is fab.

Katie Whorton (Vickers) Apologies for not sharing any news probably for at least twenty years now! Time has flown. I've been married for eleven years and Justin and I have two gorgeous (and lively!) children, Thomas (7) and Lucy (5). I work full time at Mastercard as director of partnerships and operations in the U.K/Ireland marketing department. We still do a lot of sailing, and kids are keeping us busy with football, tennis, singing, drama and running. I've continued to run for enjoyment, but last year got a place through the ballot to run the London Marathon, so more serious running kicked in again since 1997 and 1998 when I ran my first two marathons. I am running London again this year. In my fortieth year I may as well - this will be my last... at least for another twenty years

Section 63 (1994)
Section Representative:
Belle Morton

Francesca Bell (Mercer) James and I are content with country life in Suffolk with our two, Samuel (5) and Sophia (4).

Bryonie Clarendon (Leask) Living in Hampshire with George and the three boys, Edward, Freddie and Cosmo.

Victoria Edwards (Holland) We moved to Oxfordshire from London finally a couple of years ago and discovered Westonbirt old girls are everywhere. **Cordelia Gover (Harris),** two years above us, lives down the road, and two of our girls are classmates! Otherwise I am continuing enjoying being a lawyer in Mayfair although not enjoying the hellish commute. 2016 was a tricky year as I was diagnosed with lymphoma but am now in remission so 2017 so far has been much better apart from losing my hair!

Lucy Fey (Clark) I have been married to Fran for twelve years now (where does time go?!) and we have ten-year-old identical twin girls, Winnie and Belle, and a new puppy, Aggie. I live in Bristol and this year I left teaching (after more than seventeen years!) to concentrate full time on my new business as a hypnotherapist and NLP practitioner. I help adults and children with issues such as anxiety, confidence and phobias, and I love it as much as I loved teaching. I feel very lucky to be able to say I enjoy my life as well as my work! I'm looking forward to the summer where we spend lots of time camping in Devon and France.

Alyx Gerrards (Swain) I am still living near Manchester with my husband and two children, an eleven-year-old boy and an eight-year-old girl. I also run my own HR consultancy and spend my time working and taxi-ing the kids to football, lacrosse, cricket and various parties.

Jess Ingham (Hipwood) Living in Bristol with husband and two kids, Max and Emilia. Working for Orange (still) but recently joined the global brand team as their creative and digital identity manager, so working with over eighty countries where Orange is present, advising on applying the brand, lots of travel to Paris and beyond.

Nancy Lawson (White) George (10) and Zara (9) are growing up too fast, and I am still running Fawlty Towers and small meetings at Overtown! Please pop in if you are passing, love to see you.

Mary McCarthy (Oakes) Still running my little art business, MM Contemporary Arts Ltd, trading in street and contemporary art privately and hosting two auctions a year in Paris. Recently did a TEDx Talk on street art, probably the most nerve-racking experience, but if you want to see my ugly mug and watch me rabbiting on about art, then plug in! On a personal note, I'm getting married later this year so will be changing my name again and I'm living in Cheltenham with my lovely husband to be and three gorgeous boys, one is mine and the other two are my partner's, so I am way outnumbered in my household! Anyway if any of you are living in Cheltenham or venturing near this way it would be lovely to hear from you.

Belle Morton Still living in Hong Kong but moved company to KPMG Consulting. Regularly see on my travels **Ruth**, **Jemima**, **Bryonie**, **Sharifa**, **Tory Edwards** and **Clare Cameron**. I loved having Clare come and visit in Hong Kong for her birthday, and was also pleased to catch up with **Natasha Ravanello** in Mallorca this year. Hope to be able to get back to see more of you at the reunion if it happens!

Jessica O'Brien Currently living in Warwickshire and working in Leamington Spa for the Regulator of the Landfill Communities Fund, supporting local community and environment projects. Very different to media and can't believe it's been more than ten years since I left the BBC! I have recently adopted a stray farm cat, or rather she has adopted me! Other than that, enjoying travelling as much as I can and last year finally got to Florence, after twenty years of having it at the top of my list.

Sharifa Parker (Taylor) I have been working for the same IT company now for the last four years, in HR. My two girls are now seven and nine. I'm now working full time, which I enjoy most of the time. I'm definitely not the parent who spends hours on the World Book Day costume or remembers to bake cakes for the school. The girls have turned out OK though, and manage to turn up to school on time so it must be going well! I can't believe it has been thirty years since Sedgwick.

Ruth Penfold (Baker) We have moved back to UK, have a happy and healthy family, saw **Bada** and **Belle** at Christmas. Would love to see everyone if we manage to get a reunion together.

Section 62 (1993)
Section Representative:
Joanna Runcimann

No news this year.

Section 61 (1992)
Section Representative:
Caroline Walker

Coquita Mills (Marsh) No real news with me. Very much enjoying being a mother though I am sure that will change when Cecily starts school in the autumn with her brother. I saw **Corks Harris** last year, which was very nice, she was all grown up! Otherwise, I have seen **Virginia (Kelly)** and **Henrietta Burton (Evans)** though not much. Will try and do a free diving record or astronaut training for next year's entry!

Andrea Stanley My latest news is that I am moving back to Cheshire this July after nearly fifteen years in Malta. So up to my eyeballs in boxes, finding a home and a new school for Alex. Will be setting up my own business, designing mountain and diving holidays, primarily focusing on families with children who are planning their first trip with kids. Hopefully that should be in progress of beginning 2018.

Caroline Walker I'm still working as a child and adolescent psychotherapist at the Reading branch for the national charity, Survivors Trust. I am working with three-to-seventeen-year-olds and learning lots of new techniques to help children suffering from trauma. Still loving the work and my inspiring clients. I have been keeping in touch with **Charlie (Hunt), Corks (Harries), Caroline (Pullin)** and **Claire (Dorman).**

Section 60 (1991)
Section Representative:
Rebecca Willows

No news this year.

Section 59 (1990)
Section Representative:
Julia Roberts (Stubblefield)

No news this year.

Section 58 (1989)
Section Representative:
Natasha McLeod (Marsh)

Natasha McLeod (Marsh) Our younger daughter, Flora, started school in September, and I began a part-time parish admin job. I feel life has reached a healthy balance with the combination of the job, volunteering at our local primary school, playing tennis and the family. Having said that, I am toying with the idea of doing a PGCE and starting a new career in secondary education.

Susie Nash (Levitt) Andrew and I emigrated to Australia eighteen years ago. Since arriving in 1999, Andrew and I have lived in nine houses, moved for work three times (we spent three years in New Zealand) and had three children. We are now in Perth, Western Australia, and settled - for now. Our children are growing up way too quickly – Alexandra is fourteen, Olivia is twelve and Harry is nine.

I went back to university to convert my English literature degree into a teaching qualification in 2014. After ten years as a mum at home, it took some adjusting, and I am now a high-school English teacher at a state school. The job doesn't come without its challenges, but now into my third year of teaching I think I am getting the hang of it! I am forever thankful for those teachers who inspired me to follow the English path: **Mrs Thombs** and **Ms Davies**. My parents still live in Portugal and in the same house. Since we have lived this side of the world, they have come to visit every year, apart from the years we went over to visit. We visit when we can, but five return tickets from Perth requires some saving and planning. Sadly, that means that I don't see as much of **Kirstie** and **Charlotte** as I would like.

Rachel Tyler (Crone) Having lived abroad, teaching science for many years, I arrived in London in 2001 where I met my husband James. I now run my own Pilates and therapy business in and around Wimbledon and have a working life that fits in more easily with my three children. Sophie goes to secondary school in September and Oliver and Sam, my twin boys, are in Year 4.

Section 57 (1988)
Section Representative:
Fiona Stokes (Tobin) - (Section 45)

Patricia Gauci Having left the Army after twenty years, I now work as the registrar of Elstree School (Woolhampton, near Reading). It is close to home, so it is nice not to have to commute very far or move house every few years! Kat is now thirteen and Alex nine. It is nice to keep in touch with friends from school through Facebook.

Jenny Watson (Stubbs) Still living in the wonderful "real capital" of Ireland, Cork! Took some time off work at the beginning of the year to have a hysterectomy, but am now back at full pelt since. We're off to Chicago for a family christening in a couple of weeks, then to hear Phil Collins in Paris in June (I've always loved him!), and then to our timeshare in Mallorca in July/August. My husband John undertook another Ironman last year in Galway, but is now looking at ultra-marathons as he gets closer to fifty! My rheumatoid arthritis is still causing problems, and I am a veritable pin cushion injecting myself twice weekly, and having joint injections every few months. Still, the search for a cure goes on around the world.

I'm not singing as much this year, but was in London (staying with **Rachel Cairns**) last May to sing Verdi's *Requiem* in the Royal Albert Hall, and then I sang three consecutive nights with Katherine Jenkins last December, here in Cork, which was fabulous! Our son, James, managed to get a place at the Cork City School of Music to study piano and musicianship, and is just coming to the end of his first academic year with them. The facilities there are purpose-built, and he's blown away by it all.

We had to bring my late father's piano over to Cork, and I'm loving playing it again. I'm just glad to see the music genes continuing strongly in the family. Our daughter, Emma, will take Junior Cert (GCSE equivalent) in June 2018, so this is the last summer holiday that she will get three months off (yes really, in secondary school they get three months! !) for a couple of years. As a family, we'll be up with the sparrows in May, to do a sponsored walk called Darkness into Light to support suicide prevention. It starts at 4.15am!

Section 56 (1987)
Section Representative:
Fiona Stokes (Tobin) - (Section 45)

Arabella Bishop Living in Dublin and working for Sothebys still, with lots of travelling in Ireland, UK and USA!

Georgina Busch (Bryon) Still living in Stockholm. Family all enjoying the outdoor life over here, including the dog and the cat! It's been a long winter, with plenty of cross-country skiing opportunities for my husband Mikael and youngest son Noah (for whom it was his first season and he really enjoyed it), while my eldest Daniel and I stuck to the tried and tested alpine while on our spring sports holiday. After a long spell of cold weather we are looking forward to the arrival of summer and to longer days, barbecuing in the garden, fishing with the boys and exploring the archipelago further!

Victoria Calder Getting married to Neil Bastin on 29th April in Sidcup, so a little crazy with planning this as he only proposed at the end of December. Sorry to hear news of **Mr Nickols'** passing.

Juliet Davidson I am living in London and spent the first couple of months of this year focusing on a challenge across Costa Rica raising money for Cancer Research UK. Managed to raise £4,500, thanks to overwhelming support from so many people. I even played a game of cricket against the Costa Rica cricket team (yes, there is such a thing) - my first game of cricket despite having worked in cricket administration for seventeen years!

Sarah Harris-Burland Still work for the Royal Bank of Scotland in Isle of Man - twenty-one years now! Natasha is now at high school and enjoying it. Alexander is doing well and studying mathematics with the year above. Both children are learning to play the guitar.

Elizabeth Warner (Glen) Married to Bob, hubby of twenty-three years. Sounds such a long time! My eldest daughter, Emily, is nearly twenty-five. She's in her final year at university. She initially started reading history, but is now studying psychology.

Sophie would have turned twenty-one this year had she been with us. Instead, she is fifteen and always will be. We are committed to remembering Sophie with love and trying to make a difference in her name. The last year has been challenging and awful. The coroner refused to hold an inquest. Mistakes were made in treating Sophie, which we found out about through a Freedom of Information application. We also found out that when the hospital rang us six weeks after Sophie died to offer an appointment, it was not a mistake. They knew she was dead and rang us to cover themselves, after seeking legal advice. It has come to light that if we had been living near Melbourne, Sophie would almost certainly still be alive. We are distraught and broken by this. We are working with one of our federal MPs to encourage greater funding for and awareness of epilepsy. (Funding is woeful). We are also trying to create a drama award at her school in memory of Sophie.

I'm still President of the Compassionate Friends in South Australia. The group supports bereaved parents and siblings, and was started by Canon Simon Stephens in the UK in 1969. Emily started a group for the brothers and sisters. We introduced a program to support families in the country who are currently very isolated. I am hoping to return to teaching in the coming months.

We rescued a dog this year. Neglect and abuse of animals crushes my heart and faith in humanity. Despite being starved of food, affection and attention for the first fifteen months of her life, she is now thriving. She came to us on Boxing Day, sent by Sophie.

Sadly I don't remember the Headmaster well but I send my most sincere condolences to his family.

Section 55 (1986)
Section Representative:
Fiona Stokes (Tobin) - (Section 45)

No news this year.

Sections 53 and 54 (1983-5)
Section Representative:
Sarah Clunie

No news this year.

Sections 51 and 52 (1981 and 1982)
Section Representative:
Lizzie Mobbs (Overton)

No news this year.

Section 50 (1980)
Section Representative:
Lou Walker (Foord)

Marianne Aston Still living in central London and enjoying the buzz. Work as a freelance occupational psychologist keeps me busy, with frequent trips abroad and up and down the UK. Last year I ran assessment centres for various clients in Twickenham rugby stadium, Old Trafford and Stanford Bridge football grounds which was fun. Am also working as a courtesy car driver for the Wimbledon tennis championship, so the sporting theme continues. Can't say who I've had in the back of my car though! Other than work, my main commitment is with the English Chamber Choir and its full schedule of concerts and recordings. Last month we sang backing vocals at a Procol Harum gig at the Festival Hall. 'Whiter Shade of Pale' always takes me back to those sixth form discos at Clifton College! I meet up with **Christine Watts** when I'm in Cambridge, and recently had the pleasure of a month in Australia where it was great to catch up with **Kate Marchbank** and **Catherine Zuill**.

Antonia Doggart (Ross) Simon and I have decided at last to step down from running Caldicott in July 2017. He was diagnosed with renal cancer last August, he had an op to remove his left kidney, but we found out in January that the cancer had spread. He is on a course of targeted biological therapy which means two pills a day with the aim of suppressing further spread. We are upbeat, living healthily as much as we can, and are determined to enjoy our final few months of running a busy prep school before we embark on new ventures and settle down at our house at the seaside in East Wittering.

The kids are no longer kids, now aged twenty-four, twenty-two and twenty, and they are all happy in their own lives of work and play – Clare with her events business in London and the Home Counties, Charlie is putting up marquees in Hong Kong ready for the Hong Kong Sevens before travelling to Australia while he decides what he wants to do, and James (in his second year at Edinburgh) has just returned from a week's tutoring of a young boy in Denmark.

I am keeping my sanity with lots of walking the dog, some pilates, and lots of yoga and breathing (try yin yoga if you have not already!)

Tanya Hart (Gee) We currently live in Sammamish, thirty minutes from downtown Seattle, Washington. We moved here from Chicago about two years ago and love it. Much closer to our family and friends on the west coast, where we lived for many years. I have sold the licensing rights to our latest wine market brand, MeGusta Sangria, and started a new company last year in cannabis. We do marketing and branding mainly on the medicinal side emphasizing health benefits and additionally broker industrial hemp. It's been the most exciting and rewarding change of careers. We focus primarily on sustainable, circular economy manufacturing using industrial hemp, replacing typical commodities like plastics, concrete, graphene and carbon fiber with sustainable solutions using hemp. (www.titanhemp.net). We also create brands which can impact health issues, with high CBD concentrates (no THC).

As we get older, it's been hard to see the changes and health issues affecting us all. I lost my dearly beloved mum three years ago to lung cancer (she never smoked) and my father just this past year. The impact (as I'm sure many of us know) on losing our parents is heart-rending. My children, thank god, are healthy and thriving. Our daughter Gabriella is nineteen and ending her first year at university, where she also plays soccer (football). Our son is at boarding school in Carlsbad, CA and will be entering sixth form equivalent this August. He plays American football and lacrosse.

Would love to hear more of what you all are doing, if we can manage a get together it would be lovely.

Lou Walker (Foord) All well here in the Walker house. Jack's at university in Leeds and is also a personal trainer, Charlie is ostensibly doing English at Bristol but is mainly acting, singing, directing, producing and orchestra-ing, and husband Simon's new passion is paramotoring – flying round the country with a parachute overhead and a motor on his back. By the time you read this, we will have returned from (survived) an adventure travelling eight hundred miles across Morocco on monkey bikes. Neither of us is a biker. I am terrified, but looking forward to a break from my MSc in Obesity in Weight Management and forgetting for a couple of weeks that I have a research project to conduct and write up by the end of August.

Tracey Wilson (Dawes) I have left work and moved to Spain to live. Absolutely petrified about the prospect and very emotional but hey... I have been with my man Nigel and commuting between Litchfield near Birmingham for nearly three years, so time for us to do something different - and we sure are. Am keeping my house and car in London but off to see if the grass is greener on the other side. Obviously it won't be greener because of the sun, but the Mediterranean diet may well suit. We will look for work and enjoy each other's company. I also want to write, so beware everyone! Time is short and we have no idea what is around the corner so doing it while we can. So I keep telling myself! I would love to see anyone if they are down my way. We are about forty minutes from Malaga and have three bedrooms. Please feel welcome to drop in anytime.

Kate Wood (Oura) I think I mentioned that in June I was diagnosed with primary breast cancer, so have spent the year fighting that. I had a mastectomy in August and that has been followed by chemotherapy. I had the last dose in February. Radiotherapy beckons and herceptin injections for a year. It is not a nice road but has to be done. I am looking forward to not feeling nauseous, not feeling tired, enjoying a glass of wine, having hair and going on holiday! Yes that's my advice - enjoy life while you can! You never know what's round the corner.

Section 49 (1979)
Section Representative:
Fiona Merritt

Mary Ashworth (Moriarty) A very full year with the birth of our first grandson, Joel Nathaniel, in July. A great joy to have him living with us at present, along with our daughter Ruth and son-in-law Aidan. Our son, Dan, started his first graduate engineering job at Hoare Lea in Kings Cross last Easter, got engaged and married, and bought a flat within five months, treating us to a December wedding with a Korean flavour. Yva is an artist, and they are expecting a honeymoon baby in September! Our youngest daughter, Rachel, is currently working on a year-long internship at CAP

(Christians Against Poverty), which is based in Bradford. Rob continues as CEO of a small Christian charity based in Camden/Soho/London Wall, which I also work from home for, for a few hours each week. I combine this with looking after my elderly mother who has Alzheimer's and has reached the point of having no short-term memory whatsoever. We finally feel like we are seeing the end of a long probate for Rob's parents, although it will take years to get everything finalised - but we are able to enjoy one benefit in the form of a holiday rental home in Devon! We celebrated our thirtieth wedding anniversary in September and also dipped our toes (so to speak) into narrow-boating which was a wonderful, and to be repeated, activity!

Neelam Christie (Gunther) Enjoying life and very much live for my holidays! Still skiing and sailing. Jon and I have been busy visiting places such as the Amalfi coast and the Isle of Wight. This year will add an oldie twist and try my first cruise along the Croatian coast. It is good to see that WB has so many interesting events going on throughout the year. I will endeavour to fit one in.

Alison Kerby (Wilson) Everything is trundling along in the Kerby household. Georgie is nearly half way through her training contract with a solicitors' practice in High Wycombe; she is about to transfer to their London office so is currently flat hunting. Olly is about to go travelling for a few months prior to going to Sandhurst in September. Fraser is over halfway through his second lambing which is going well. Rob and I are still working at the 'day job', as well as being assistant lambers when required. We are hoping to find time for a holiday in the not too distant future, but not holding our breath!

Joanna Kidson (Rowson) 2017 has been a busy year. Bex (turning twenty-one at the end of the year) has started her third year of sociology and geography, managing to maintain excellent grades whilst also enjoying the flatting life. Jono (turns eighteen in the middle of the year) is in his final year of school; he seems to be settling on engineering for the next step with a decision to make on Auckland (for the sailing) or Christchurch (for the skiing)! Philip continues to provide electricity for the Central North Island, and I continue to keep busy, despite a plan for more part-time work as the kids left home, so Philip could drop some hours and we could spend some time travelling around New Zealand (and maybe the world!)

Unfortunately a downturn in Philip's parents' health has meant that my care commitments have moved from the lower generation to the upper generation, and changes within my clients have led to more work rather than less for now. I continue as treasurer for the church we attend and do an afternoon stint at the Op Shop too. We have had a steady stream of twenty-somethings visiting from the northern hemisphere which has been great. We have also just completed a ten-week renovation project that took six months, so the house is once again available for any visitors venturing south.

Joan Lowton (Mullens) We have moved down to Hampshire. Andrew got a job here first, then I got one, and then we found a circa-1900 house and moved in early November. Both enjoying new location and jobs and continuing our travels. Just back from Costa Rica and Nicaragua, which were great, but very different countries, incredible as they are smack next door to each other. I'm going for a very quick trip to Australia, for my sister's sixtieth birthday, as a surprise along with my mum, other sister and brother. At eighty-six, Mum is going to stay on for another week, as she doesn't feel that her body could cope with less than a week there, hoping mine can!

Fiona Merritt Still hoping to "catch up" but unsure will succeed – work, Specials, trying to keep less unfit, home, diving, skiing, family and friends still feature, with technical fault delay on last year's Red Sea trip resulting in a nice refund that covered long weekend skiing in Switzerland this year. Wishing had not started digging over front garden, an on-going project that upsets my back and knees. Caught up with **Marguerite Williams** when over recently, experimenting with pesto mash topping for fish pie – no adverse reactions reported, but you won't see me on MasterChef!

Nicola Tehel (Palmer) Alive and busy, living the holiday that is Devon life! Visiting NHS EMI (Elderly Mentally Infirm) units with Lulu, the registered Pets As Therapy dog, who has just turned one.

Marguerite Williams (Morris) I have just received notice that I am now a CISA – Certified Information Systems Auditor - which is internationally recognized. Still bemused that at my age, my career seems to have gone into restart, with becoming a CPA and a CISA within the last two years. I am currently very much enjoying working for a California-based CPA firm as part of a small team working on IT assurance. The amount of travel is considerably more reasonable than my previous employer, though I miss the benefits of air miles and hotel points. We are traveling to the UK more frequently to visit my mother and her husband as they age gracefully. This is also an opportunity to catch up with my daughter who has settled in Edinburgh. Our son graduates from Cal-Poly in June and will be moving home, to start working for Amazon locally. Still wish that US-based employers had more reasonable leave arrangements. If anyone is coming to the Bay area, do consider stopping by.

Section 48 (1978)
Section Representative:
Amiel Price

Hoping to hold a reunion next year – forty years since our section left in 1978. Please contact me or the school if you are interested in joining us, and please spread the word, as I know there are more of you out there than are sending in news!

Johanna Justice Not much to report, still living in Cornwall and still working on the house and having the final windows replaced soon so I shall be fully double glazed. Travelled to Malta in November last year which was beautiful and educational. Then it's off to India next year for a once-in-a-lifetime trip to follow in my grandparents' footsteps, when my grandfather was out in India in the army during the 1920s, to see the Golden Triangle, Ranthambore (jeep safaris to see the elusive Tiger), and up to Shimla on the toy train.

Susan Kennedy (Sheard) The last year has been busy, I was very proud to have run my fourteenth marathon last April with the least training due to injury and joint aches (from my cancer drugs), but I did it and raised money for a friend who died. My job has been really full on as we bought a big company and I had to oversee the integration of the CRM system and about sixty people onto the new system. It was a mad few weeks.

My dear husband has been appearing as the friendly Scottish chef in *The Halcyon* and then embarrassing the children in a cameo role in *Trainspotting T2* with no clothes on in a very compromising position! I went to the première and hid behind my hands.

Our eldest, James, has been working for two years now in digital marketing at Xaxis doing data analysis, and our youngest, Patrick, is at Bristol in his final fourth year studying maths and philosophy. He has a two-year working visa for Canada set up for when he graduates – a girlfriend and a job beckon! I keep in touch with some old friends via the power of Facebook, **Nicky, Angie** also we try and meet up sometimes with **Gillie, Fee, Claire and Cally**. Also I see **Rachel (Nobes)** once or twice a year when she and her girls come to London for a trip. I am still running and hope to complete the Manchester marathon this April, body permitting!

Joanna Melhuish (Marchbank) Simon and I are still in Barnes, London, with the four children over eighteen and spread around the world. Tom is a doctor in Wagga Wagga, Australia. I was lucky enough to go visit him and his partner d'Arcy in January this year. Ella and her boyfriend have saved up and escaped London media work to go travelling for a year round the world. Max is studying for a physics degree in Bristol, so is near enough to visit. When I get my act together, I hope to see **Amelia (Trevethick)** on the way there or back. We keep trying to hatch a plan and now I just have to do it! After twenty-five years with kids at school, Mia leaves this summer to have a breather, and I have stopped working in schools, so after a lifetime linked to term times, we will be a liberated family!

We see the Harveys **(Charlotte Edgar)** and their four grown-ups (can't say kids any more) as often as we can. I think the summer meet-up will be in Cornwall this year. Let's hope the weather is kind.

My sister **Kate** is over now and again, having married a Pom second time round and moving from Sydney to Noosa for a bit, I think, next year. And she is in touch with **Catherine Zuill**, when they are both in Sydney. I know she enjoys catching up with old Westonbirt friends when she gets over to England, too.

Amiel Price We had a quiet celebration for Dad's 90th birthday last year with neighbours and family. My brother, no longer having a dog to care for, spent a lot of the year on walking holidays and made a whole new set of friends. I've made new friends where I volunteer at Singleton Park with the Friends of Swansea Botanic Gardens. We grow and sell plants to the public. At present we are raising funds for a wildflower and wellbeing area with paths suitable for wheelchair and pram access. I have just been made 'head of herbs'!

My main project at present keeps me busy typing up WW1 letters written to my Grandmother by her fiancé who got killed on the Eastern Front (Jerusalem). He wrote to her every other day, and with extracts from his diary and also from hers, plus his cartoon drawings and a few photographs, it all makes for interesting reading and I hope to publish them in due course.

Oh, and I have a cat from the local rescue home to keep me company, which is a novelty for me but delightful. I love dogs, but at the moment a cat suits me and Dad. They enjoy similar activities: sitting about and snoozing!

Earlier this year I met up with **Lorraine Stanton (Martin)**, **Charlotte Walpole**, **Sarah Hamilton (Addams-Williams)** and **Polly Davies**, which was great fun. I also keep in touch with **Amelia Trevethick**, **Sallie Robertson**, **Jane Tompsett (Hunter)**, and **Alicia Holmes (Rolston)**, **Rachel McFarlane** and **Liz White**.

Stephanie Wolfe (Binder) In haste as I am just about to go to New York with our oldest son. Alex developed a very rare condition for twenty-four-year olds last summer called pulmonary hypertension which is usually a condition people develop when they are much older. As he lay very ill in St Thomas' Hospital waiting to be diagnosed and treated I promised to take him to New York when he got better as he has always wanted to go. As his illness has arisen spontaneously and not as a complication of something else, this makes him interesting and his specialists were delighted to find out quite how many siblings and first cousins he has as they are interested in the genetics!

The gardening business keeps me and three other regular staff busy and we have no trouble finding work. The ageing population means that there are always lots of people who need their gardens tidied and their grass cut. We have also been doing more work involving design. I am not going to make my fortune doing this, but it is enjoyable, especially with a great bunch of ladies who never allow me to take myself too seriously. I am also still very active as a lay minister taking services and helping to run Messy Church in our rural benefice. My husband Simon still works part-time as a solicitor and part-time as a notary, and his two beehives keep us in honey. We play string quartets together with friends once a month very badly and sing with different choirs.

Rebecca our eldest broke up from her boyfriend before Christmas and has taken her broken heart off to Athens where she is working for subsistence pay and volunteering as an interpreter; she did Arabic and Farsi at university. Heaven knows if/when she will ever return as she has taken Brexit hard.

Flo, after two years working as a researcher for a Royal Household, is shortly going back to work as a land agent and has recently with our help bought a maisonette in Penge with Alex who is working in PR.

Alan is in his last year at Cardiff reading ancient history and archaeology and is meant to be job hunting.

PS the ducks and chickens are still going strong, but the menagerie has reduced to two tortoises, one dog and one cat.

Section 47 (1977)
Section Representative:
Fiona Leith

Henrietta Ewart My news is that I have moved to the Isle of Man to take up the post of director of public health. I'm just moving in to my new home in Peel and looking forward to spring to do a bit more exploring of the wonderful countryside here.

Cherry James (Lucas) We are all fine; I continue working at London South Bank University, though the result of the referendum adds considerable and most unwelcome uncertainty to the life of a lecturer in EU law, as it does to those working in UK higher education generally. The whole sorry debacle has made me politically active for the first time in my life - maybe I shouldn't have left it so late! Last year saw both children in Europe. Anna was working in Paris for a year after graduation. She is now back in London training to be a chartered surveyor and living at home (just lovely), though may go back to Paris, once qualified, if possible. Freddie is still engaged in postgraduate studies in organ and harpsichord at the music school in Stuttgart, and doing an increasing amount of freelance work there as well as a part-time job as a church organist. He hopes to stay on in that part of the world.

Freddie's life in southern Germany has had the most welcome by-product for us of enjoying seeing **Nicky Vollkommer (Sperry)** who lives not far from Stuttgart.

Nicky organised a most wonderful English style Festival of Nine Lessons and Carols at the beautiful Marienkirche in Reutlingen just before Christmas last year, and Freddie played the organ for the service. Simon and I went out for the weekend and what a wonderful time we had, especially as Nicky's daughter, Jessica, chose to get married on the very next day, and we were honoured to be invited to the service and to the memorable German-Christmas-market-style reception afterwards. It was a splendid weekend.

Over the year I have also enjoyed seeing **Henrietta Ewart** and **Corinna Kershaw (Chown)** on number of occasions. As for me, I managed my fourth London Marathon last April. I can't say it's got any easier, but if you remember my [total lack of] sporting prowess at WB, you will appreciate the kick I get out of saying that I have now run four marathons!

Serena Jones (Walthall) My life has got busier in the last six months. Dave retired from Rolls Royce, and he's now got more time for holidays and is coming up with ideas of things we can do together. Over the next few months we have holidays planned in Spain, Sardinia and Greece, and all out of season now that our youngest has left school: three holidays for the price of the normal one in August, which is welcome. We also have several short breaks and courses planned, and are visiting Dave's parents (aged ninety-nine and ninety-one) more often than we used to.

My woodwork skills are progressing nicely. Anyone who has visited me will have been shown my pride and joy: an open-topped kindling box with dovetails down each corner, made completely with hand tools – saws, planes and chisels – and with wood from our own woods in Herefordshire, which is particularly satisfying. I'm now making a shelving unit, made to measure for a particular space.

Still involved with WB Association, I held a 'bring and share' lunch at our house in March for anyone who lives in or near Bristol. We had five people here all from different eras, but we all remembered **Miss Venning**, **Major Millman**, **Miss Vanstone** and others! Many of the local people who couldn't make that date seemed interested in coming to another do, so I may do something else some time. If anyone else thinks they might have enough people living nearby to hold a regional event, I can help get you started (get my contact details from **Alison Salih** at the school and also ask her for a list of people in your area). Looking forward to our forty-year reunion in October and hope lots of people will come.

Sally Kincaid (Franklin) Another year and another new job, still in health, but for the first time venturing outside general practice and into a whole new area. I've taken on the chief exec role with Australian Society for medical imaging and radiation therapy, which I am absolutely loving. Ten weeks into the job at the time of writing, and I have just returned from a week in Perth for our annual conference, AGM and two-day face-to-face board and expert panel meetings. I was pretty knackered by the end, but also incredibly excited about the work ahead with this organisation. There's a fair bit of international conference attendance and travel attached this year too: Ottowa in April, Manchester in June (which will enable me to spend a few days with my parents in Shropshire too), Hong Kong in June, Nelson (NZ) in August and Chicago in November, plus a pretty heavy schedule of transcontinental travel in Australia, all of which I love, despite my dear husband's frequent refrain of "don't you think you are too old for all this travel?" Pah!

Talking of 'too old', Andrew at the age of sixty continues to run regularly and competitively – regular 20kms at the weekends and a variety of distances and training during the week, interspersed with the odd half marathon race. He regularly has 'podium finishes' such as last weekend at the Hanging Rock race (first in his age group – the over-sixties, but more impressively, he came second in the over-fifties age group). He's loving his role at the civil and administrative tribunal – a mixture of instant justice *Judge Judy* style rulings and long five-to-ten-day complex building and other issues.

Jack completed his BA at the end of 2015, majoring in government and international relations and history, then worked for an overseas aid and development agency for twelve months, but has now decided to do post-grad law so has gone back to uni to do his JD. Sadly he's decided to do this in Sydney, so we don't see as much of him as we would like – it's an eight-hour drive or ninety-minute flight.

Last year Andrew and I had our first proper holiday together in the UK for about fifteen years. Usually it's just me popping over for family visits, but this time we had a week in Trebethowick, Cornwall (**Penny Sloman (Sheard)** came and spent some time with us there which was brilliant), followed by a week fell walking and eating amazingly in the Lake District, where I spent many of my childhood holidays with grandparents. A highlight was our stay at Sharrow Bay on Ullswater, and for me standing in the shadow of Blencathra, which I had first climbed when I was about fourteen. Sadly didn't have the opportunity to climb it this time, but it will still be there for another assault sometime in the future. Holiday plans this year include being in the UK in October for the fortieth reunion at Westonbirt, which I'm really looking forward to, and some time in Portugal and the Orkneys – at least that's the current plan. So in essence, the Kincaids carry on apace – lots of little news, no big news, and an open door for anyone travelling our way.

Fiona Leith (Goodbody): We found a week last summer when all the children were free and spent it together in Copenhagen and Stockholm, which none of us had visited before. Lovely cities and we especially enjoyed the Vasa (think Mary Rose, but complete) in Stockholm.

Then we had another wonderful Goodbody family gathering in August to see **Jennifer's** (**Goodbody** Section 44) daughter Cara getting married. I have endured a particularly challenging six months in my role as chair of governors at our village school, but thankfully that is now in the past. We did manage to sneak away for a holiday in St Lucia to soak up some winter vitamin D, which is probably the only reason I am still sane. I have taken up agility training with my labrador. Its great fun and forces both of us to concentrate hard. She is rather better at it than me and often stops and looks at me with a massive question mark over her head, wondering what on earth I am asking her to do next, as I try to disentangle my arms and legs to give the right signal.

Lovely to see so many of our year group at the AGM in the autumn, and I hope lots more are able to make it this October to mark the forty years since leaving. What a thought!

Gloriana Marks de Chabris Eighteen months ago I set up a new business converting commercial buildings into high-end apartments under the brand Urban Revolution (I came up with the name when we were on vacation in NYC last summer as it seemed to suit the business!) I am just completing the first development of four apartments in the heart of Winchester, to be followed by five houses near Alton in Hampshire, and then a third development of five listed apartments in Surrey. So far, so good! I have been approached by developers and investors who want to work with me on some new-build developments and larger conversion sites so it could be the start of an interesting next career. Who knows? Meanwhile, I have entrusted my residential lettings business to a team of staff who have worked for me for years. Having a lot to do certainly keeps the grey matter going!

Graeme has recently joined the board of IFAW (International Fund for Animal Welfare) whose mission is to rescue and protect animals around the world. Everyday there is another sad story (eg Trump and climate change) or a wonderful success (eg project to protect manatees) on their website. He was very proud to be asked and looking forward to the many challenges!

Rosella is now at college doing her A Levels, having done worlds better in her GCSEs than her mother did in her O Levels all those years ago. Next stop is university. How time flies!

On that subject, how can it be forty years since we left? I hope we can get a reunion organised.

Wendy McWilliams Hard to believe it is forty years since we left school and really do not feel fundamentally different despite the occasional grey hair, extra pound or two and joints that are not quite as supple as they used to be. Still, refused to be cowed by age, going skiing very soon and have every intention of starting early and staying out on the slopes as long as possible, followed by lightweight après-ski which will probably involve a lovely meal and an early night. The kids can hit the Irish bar till the wee small hours.

Still have three on the pay roll, probably another three years of that so very little prospect of retirement. They lost their father in 2015 in a tragic road accident (sudden, brutal and traumatic), so it has been a very difficult couple of years coping with that and has not been easy but they are pulling through. Hope we are old enough to moan about the youth, but their complete inability to grasp the concept of a map amazes me, could not navigate out of a paper bag without a phone and satnav. One told a university friend that she lived in Bedford, south of London. Another realised that after leaving central London to go to Liverpool, he just might possibly be going the wrong way when he arrived in East Sheen. My history student thought it would be a lovely idea to visit Waterloo but wondered why I was talking about a Eurostar to Brussels, why didn't we just go to London, "It's near Trafalgar Square, Mum". All that money on education, can I ask for my money back? Hope all well with everyone.

Tina Panton (Galanis) Still loving living in Symi in all weathers but especially in winter when there's no-one around. This is probably the third year that I've said "the house is nearly finished" - the long day wears on! The garden is due to be planted next weekend. So perhaps the end really is in sight. Then I can start redecorating the parts we finished two years ago!

Here's something unexpected for you all - I've stopped drinking alcohol. No fags no alcohol. My life as I know it is over! But I' m enjoying feeling well again after feeling crap for nearly all last year. They still haven't identified what has been wrong with me, but who cares? I feel better!

Animal contingent has increased again - again down to our eldest. Last autumn she presented me with three kittens the night before she left to live in Barcelona. Poor old Dave has never liked cats! So we now have one dog and five cats. Crazy cat lady on the corner is my new nickname.

Love and best wishes to all my fellow fifty-eight-year-olds and hope to see you all in October, if not before. As always, if you are in the eastern Aegean please come and see us. Xxxx

Kate Porter (Bullock) Hello Everyone! I am still teaching primary at Fallin, just outside Stirling, and continue to teach French, RME, H&W etc to upper school classes this year. It has been a challenging year in some ways, but we are keeping our heads above water! The family are all fine and my Mum, **Mrs Bullock, (Staff))** is still doing really well too at the age of ninety-seven! We go down and see her as often as we can, but it is hard not being geographically close. She is still in touch with several other former staff and sees **Diana Challis (Staff)** regularly. *(Ed: Kate submitted this news prior to the sad death of her mother shortly afterwards, and you can read her obituary towards the front of this magazine.)*

In the Easter break, Stewart and I are looking forward to a fortnight driving holiday around southern Ireland. I have fond memories of several childhood holidays there but Stewart has never been.

Good wishes to all and a warm welcome on offer to anyone who is heading to the Stirling area any time and who fancies a wee catch up!

Leigh Ralphs (Davidson) We had an amazing trip to South Africa with our boys (now twenty-nine and twenty-five) in April 2016. We spent three days in Cape Town (Table Mountain, Robben Island, Cape of Good Hope and penguins at Boulders), then drove to the wine region to stay in a vineyard, to an ostrich farm in the Klein Karoo and then through the incredible mountain passes and along the garden route to Knysna. We finished our wonderful holiday with a three-day safari and a visit to Addo Elephant Park - a brilliant time.

We had a few days in Edinburgh in May, and I visited the castle for the first time, and HMS Britannia, which was a real treat. We also managed a bit of time in Spain which is always relaxing. Unfortunately my shoulder is still "frozen" so I have had to put my golf on hold and am taking long walks instead!

We've been to the Malvern Theatre and cinema quite a lot and often pop up to London for a catch up with friends. Several sixtieth birthday invitations are making an appearance - not long now! Looking forward to celebrating our Section's fortieth Anniversary at WB on Saturday 14 October (lunch and tea) - hope as many of you as possible can make it! **Sally Kincaid (Franklin)** is in charge.

James is still loving teaching at Bryanston (newly qualified) and Charlie is moving to Lady Eleanor Holles School in September as Deputy Head of maths which he is very excited about. Guyon is still enjoying Malvern and being involved in its expansion overseas. Having built a new science centre they are now starting on a new theatre and have just opened a new water-based astro for hockey.

It was great to see **Fiona Leith (Goodbody), Fiona Dix (Bolus), Susan Wong, Serena Jones (Walthall), Jenny Webb (Binder)** and **Sue Brough (Purnell)** at the AGM at WB last October and we all went to the Memorial Service for Miss Newton in the chapel, where **Katharine Hill (Cemlyn-Jones)** gave the address.

Shortly after that and completely out of the blue, I was diagnosed with Stage 1 cancer of the uterus and had to have an urgent abdominal hysterectomy followed by a short course of radiotherapy (brachytherapy) straight after Christmas! Thankfully it was caught early and all seems to have gone well and I will continue to have three-monthly check-ups for the next few years. I was enormously grateful for the support of friends and prayer which literally carried me through quite a rollercoaster of a time. As a "reward for good behaviour", Guyon is taking me to the Maldives this weekend, which I am extremely excited about!

Nicola Vollkommer (Sperry) We've now got eight children instead of four, with a young man called Janis becoming our offspring-in-law number four after marrying Jessica, our youngest daughter, just before Christmas. We are blessed with four fantastic children-in-law, and are very grateful. So there's been another wedding, another grandbaby (Letizia Hella), another book published (for photos and updates, see www.nicola-vollkommer-buecher.de), life expanding in all directions, just when we thought it might begin to calm down. The empty house is a weird feeling, even though I appreciate finding bits of the house still clean and tidy two days after cleaning and tidying it.

One major highlight of last year was our first very English Festival of Carols in St Mary's Cathedral (Marienkirche) here in Reutlingen. A German choir (we got together a hundred singers!) singing English carols - what a sensation! And a packed cathedral, standing room only. It all began when **Cherry (Lucas)** and Simon **James** visited us the year before, and their wonderful son Freddie ended up at the church music college in Stuttgart to continue his organ studies. This development made the planning of an English carol service irresistible, and Freddie was planned in straight away as our organist. He was brilliant, and the service was so moving and unforgettable that we were asked to do it again next year. So there we are - how wonderful that friendships forged way back on the icy lacrosse fields of WB can write a piece of local history in the Southern German province 40 years later!

Jenny Webb (Binder) 2016, the year my youngest turned twenty-one, marks an end to one sort of parenting, but we are still on back up! At the other end of the age scale, I have had to step the amount of time keeping an eye on my father.

Had a super week in Tuscany with ALL the extended family in July (despite Italian traffic controllers' best efforts!) Then John and I had a week in Rome in October and for the first time ever had a city tour on a Segway - great fun. Rather ominously, Italy had earthquakes a week after each visit so may stay away for a while. Otherwise life is much the same - governor at two schools, walking, bridge, tennis, NADFAS etc. Saw some familiar faces at Association Day last October and looking forward to seeing more of our year at the fortieth reunion this October.

Section 46 (1976)
Section Representative:
Jean Stone

No news submitted this year.

Section 45 (1975)
Section Representative:
Fiona Stokes (Tobin)

Lizzie Bennett Another year has flown by. Dave, Emma and I are off to China in mid-April, a fourteen-day itinerary which includes Beijing, the Great Wall, the Terracotta Army and lots of other places which look amazing. We are also having a day volunteering at a Panda Research Centre which Emma and I are really excited about. On the way home we will be spending two days in Hong Kong.

In September this year, I will have been working at the Institute of Cancer Research (ICR) for forty years and decided in January that it's time to stop – my last working day will be 14th September.

Have seen **Fiona** during the year and heard about **Virginia** as her daughter, Emily, started work at the ICR last year and works in the same building as me. I hope to be able to catch up with more people later in the year when I have more time!

Anne Millman How quickly this beautiful time of year comes round again – I hope it finds you well. Thank you for continuing to shoulder the burden of collecting our various bits and pieces of news. Oh, what shall I write?!

My husband, Hans, and I have now been living in Blewbury for just over three years, and are continuing to delight in the surrounding countryside and the character (and characters) of such a special village. It's good to be near Oxford again, too, after so many years since my student days there, and we continue to have quite a queue of visitors wanting to come to stay. I'm keeping very busy with work, which shows no signs of slowing down at all, and includes so many interesting projects: I'm currently working on projects for the Salisbury Museum; an archaeological site called Much Fen near Peterborough; the Hendrix/Handel Museum in London; and a continued tour of Constable's great painting 'Salisbury Cathedral from the Meadows' which is just about to arrive at the National Gallery of Scotland, Edinburgh. I feel so lucky to have some stability during the ghastly and dysfunctional political context we are living in.

As I write this my family in the Netherlands are going to the polls, and I just hope balance and fairness will prevail, but I'm also looking ahead to happy occasions, with my mother's ninety-fifth birthday just around the corner, and some treats to celebrate being sixty this year, one of which is a trip to St Petersburg with **Trudy Wardle**. I hope everyone in my year also have some joyous sixtieth happenings in 2017.

Fiona Stokes (Tobin) In February 2017 I fulfilled a long-held plan to visit **Jo Grobler (Jocelyne Clarke)** in South Africa. Chris and I flew to Cape Town for a few days and visited Robben Island, the former prison of Nelson Mandela and achieved an ambition to climb to the top of Table Mountain. We then drove a hire car to Oubaai (Old Bay), near George, to stay with Jo and her husband Carl in their beautiful home on a golf estate situated between the Outeniqua mountains and the Indian Ocean. They took us with them on safari to two different national parks, Mountain Zebra and Addo Elephant, and the four of us visited the Tsitsikama nature reserve on our return journey to Oubaai. One of the highlights for me was a visit to an animal sanctuary near Oudtshoorn, where we were able to stroke a young hand-reared cheetah - a little bit scarier for me than your average household feline!

Our sons Matt and Ben are both living back at home now and working in Marlow and Bagshot respectively, Matt in IT sales and Ben in IT recruitment. Ollie is living in Ealing and working in the civil service (Medicines Regulatory Health Authority).

Spent a hilarious evening with **Ali Cheeseman (Dorey)** and **Caroline Mant (Liddiard)** and our menfolk just after Christmas at the Mants' home near Northampton.

Still periodically see **Lizzie Bennett (Phelps)**, **Clare Williams** and **Trudy Evans (Wardle)**, and managed to meet up last year with **Anne Millman** and **Jenefer Greenwood**.

Someone has to mention it – most of us are turning sixty this year. Happy birthday one and all!

Gilly Stuart Smith (Ward) After twenty years, we decided to close our farm shop, Sussex Farm Foods, in May 2016. A sad move as we had some great staff and lovely customers, but let's just blame the huge growth of the supermarkets in our area as a major factor. So I have now joined the ranks of golfers, although it seems to take me rather a long time to get round the course. Hopefully I will improve enough to get a handicap soon.

Fabian, our younger son, has left Sherborne, and having spent four months teaching in extremely rural Malawi – a very challenging location with no food, water or electricity – he is now enjoying travelling in south east Asia. He is lined up for Oxford Brookes in the autumn. Meanwhile Marcus is about to finish his chemistry degree at Newcastle and join the ranks of the unemployed! Let's hope something turns up.

Susie Younger (Goodbody) We are renovating and extending a cottage on the west coast of Scotland in order to holiday there and let out as a holiday business. The project is moving very slowly which is very frustrating as I am project managing it. Life just moves at a different speed over there so I am trying to stay calm! With the threat of yet another referendum I am wondering if we should have bought in England.

With no cows to calve this year, the farm seems strangely empty, and we are both missing them, but probably not the attached dramas that always ensued.

Still no grandchildren, but the boys are all doing fine.

Section 44 (1974)
Section Representative:
Elizabeth Battye (Jones)

Elizabeth Battye (Jones) I am enjoying retirement finding lots of different activities to keep me occupied, although my husband Chris is still working. Our daughter is getting married in June, so we are busy arranging the wedding. Our son, Thomas, lives nearby with his girlfriend, and works as an accountant locally.

Tina Cook (Jenne) Seems like a big new chapter with Steve retiring this May. He's not quite retirement age, but he feels it's the right time, and there is plenty to occupy him over the summer at the farm and in the garden etc! He's been advised not to take on any new activities for at least three months, even though he's already being asked… We're going on a three-week holiday in September, after which he will probably start getting very busy.

I'm continuing to teach piano, but probably won't take on many new students. It's a great job with maximum flexibility being self-employed, and I think all my students at the moment are super keen. We are looking forward to seeing **Carol Pusey (Cleal)** and her husband when they come to stay towards the end of April, when she is singing in the cathedral with her choir one Sunday.

Hannah continues with her medical course, and this year is doing an extra degree in international medicine, which will involve a trip to Tanzania to do some research related to AIDS.

Charlotte England (Wren) It has been a very busy year. In May 2016 we came over to Europe with friends and had a terrific trip. The Chelsea Flower Show, the First World War battlefields, mainly to find my husband's great uncle who died there in April 1917, then on to Paris, Avignon, southern France and over to Italy. We also stayed for a while with my cousins in the Dordogne. Then back to the UK for more relatives and friends. All in all, about ten weeks, which was wonderful and a great deal of fun.

In December we had **Pauline Jackson** to stay, which was lovely. She was on a trip to the Antipodes to see family and friends, so we were able to show her Melbourne and also the Mornington peninsula. It was wonderful to introduce her to a different part of the world which has been my home now for over thirty years!

This European summer, we will be back in Europe for another couple of months again to see family and friends, but also to visit our son and his wife, who live in London. They have been there for four years and are enjoying the London life. Their work is in the wine industry which takes them to all parts of Europe and the US and is a great experience for them.

Julia Goss (Willcox) In June we came back from our two-year stint in Saudi Arabia. Much to many people's surprise, including mine, I enjoyed the experience of living in such a strange place and the opportunity to travel to many Middle Eastern countries. In many ways, compound living was like Westonbirt, but with an open-air pool and wall-to-wall sunshine. As in school, I was lucky enough to make friends with people from all over the world. Arrived back in time to vote on Brexit and, without wishing to be political, I was so disappointed with the results. It is good to be home, and I am settling back into UK life. Still keep in touch with **Elspeth Weaver (Bolus)**, **Lulu James** and **Tish John (Bush)**.

Pauline Jackson (Garrett) Keeping busy all the time. Occasional work at local secondary school, invigilating and reading/scribing for exams. Several visits to home in Spain - always lots to keep me occupied there, and I do like the warmer weather. Highlight of the year; visited **Charlotte England (Wren)** in Melbourne where she has a wonderful life! Went over to New Zealand and did a nine-thousand-kilometre road trip; fabulous country, both scenery and people. Surprised my daughter (who was on holiday in New Zealand with her New Zealand partner) on Christmas Day in Wellington - she thought I was in Spain! Eldest son Stephen continues to work in electrics, Paul a film-maker, Laura works for Studio Canal film company, and youngest son David has his own business in vehicle wrapping and signage.

Tish John (Bush) It's been a busy couple of years in the **John (Bush)** household! Dave and Biff have both produced Evie and Llewelyn respectively in 2016, seven months apart. So lovely but so exhausting! Both live away so the M4 is being well worn by my car!

If anyone is doing granny duty or is at a loose end in London or near Woking anytime, I'd love to catch up with you. It's a long day and adult company for a coffee/lunch would be great while I'm away from home!

Otherwise Nick and I are good, the big sixty being fairly kind so far. Still trying to keep fit with cycling and parkrun - if you have one near you, I recommend it. The coffee afterwards is magnificent!

Went to the WB carol service last December - it was fantastic being in the Great Hall singing! (And leaving to go home afterwards!)

Section 43 (1973)
Section Representative:
Sarah Thomas (Leslie)

Thank you to all for sending in news. I myself am still enjoying my job as Financial Controller of a Japanese company in Coventry and still bell-ringing as much as I can in my spare time. Having moved house again a couple of years ago, we are now in the middle of a comprehensive extension and renovation project. Now I know why we were previously attracted by new houses. I'm looking forward to the time when the upheaval becomes a distant memory.

My sister **Jean Leslie** (Section 41) still lives in Australia and is retired now. She will be visiting for a few months later in the year.

Lorraine Clemie (Gibbs) All well with John and me. I am still working as a speech therapist part-time.

We now have three tiny grandchildren and one ready-made nineteen-year-old. The three little ones are eighteen months, six months and ten weeks. All boys and all great fun.

Our older son and his partner live next door, and the younger son and his wife are living with us whilst they wait to move into their new house nearby. We are loving having the family all together.

I got together with some WB ex-pupils last year and it was great to see old chums.

Tish Golding After nearly thirty years at the BBC World Service, I hung up my headphones at the end of December. I was sad to say goodbye to so many great people, many of whom I had worked with for years, but the time had come.

My husband, Maurice, retired last April, and it's great to be able to do things and go places without worrying about leave requests etc. That said, I found stopping work in January wasn't the best time and felt quite depressed for a while, but now spring is here, I'm raring to go. At the end of November, we went to South Africa for three weeks' holiday. It was my first trip back to Africa after some twenty-seven years away and it was great to be back. We explored the Cape and then had a week in a wildlife conservancy just outside the Kruger National Park. After two years of drought, the rains had come about three weeks previously. You could just feel the animals' happiness. We saw so much wonderful game, but the elephants were fantastic and endlessly fascinating. Even though I grew up in Kenya, I'd forgotten just how amazing it is to see these animals in their own environment. I'm not leaving it another twenty-seven years.

On the home front, our elder daughter is about to have her third baby. She lives about an hour away, so we see plenty of the grandchildren. Our son finished at Bristol University in 2015 and has done various jobs while he decides what he wants to do as a career. He's just back from two months travelling in India. He's still only twenty-two and, as he says, will probably be working until he's seventy, so I have some sympathy with his desire not to be pinned down yet. Our younger daughter has just gone to Hull University to do theatre studies.

Maurice meanwhile has devoted most of his first year of retirement to completely redesigning, digging and planting the garden and to date has done a great job. This last year I've seen a number of WB friends - **Alison Seymour-Williams, Pippa Mason, Carol Kynnersley, Zoe Littleton, Karin O'Hare, Lorrie Gibbs, Cathy Burnaby-Atkins, Jean Leslie**, and after some twenty-five years, **Rekha Ghose**, who was very briefly over from California. Zoe and I met her for lunch. She was the same gorgeous Rekha.

Zoe Littleton Retirement is great. I've just one non-exec director role for a property development company and apart from that am work-free and flitting between London and Arles.

Claire Linzee (Thomas) is still enjoying life in Saint Louis, Missouri, USA.

Section 42 (1972)
Section Representative:
Miranda Purves (Saxby-Soffe)

Jane Barrett has managed to avoid doing any actual teaching work during the past year (as although she officially retired in 2013 she kept being called back to do "a little sixth form Latin or whatever"). In compensation, she is teaching a Burmese doctor friend English, which works brilliantly as her English is already excellent and Jane has no experience of EFL!

Libby Coats (Clover) had very little news apart from being about to become a grandmother and to say that she was reading *Terms and Conditions: Life in Girls' Boarding Schools 1939-1979* by **Ysende Maxtona Graham** which contains some interesting reminders!

Rosalie Fowler (Goldingham) is finally emotionally free again having found her courage to step away from her second marriage and is now loving her retrieved single life! She is still working for Cafcass for four days a week which has provided stability. She continues to sing with Gainsborough Choral Society and plays bridge, tennis and table tennis. Her son Henry is farming in Lincolnshire; Emily and husband Seb are chartered surveyors in London, and Thomas is a finance analyst in Norwich. Rosalie was just off to a much-needed week in Mallorca with a girlfriend and also to sing and perform Vivaldi's *Gloria* and John Rutter's *Requiem* with The Really Big Chorus in the Basilica di Sant Francesc, Palma, which has taken her straight back to WB in 1971 when they sang the Gloria and also Britten's *St Nicholas* with the Boys Choir School Gloucester. What an exciting venture that was! This has also reminded her that it is about forty-five years since we all left – amazing!

Sally Gesua (Clifford) had just returned from the depths of India as they are trying to fit in travel to far-flung places before they get too decrepit! Hopefully South America next year, and Antibes is next on the list for a big bridge tournament (nice venue!) Otherwise life plods on with plenty of sport and bridge, and grandchildren appearing at regular intervals.

Diana Graham (Gantlett) again was the first to respond to the request for news, but said she would give the others a chance to reply first! However, she did give me contact details for **Louise Gordon Canning**, whom I had not heard from since we left school.

Miranda Purves (Saxby-Soffe) I am still sorting out matters in Kent and elsewhere and selling objects I no longer need. However, I am also buying objects I do not really need but cannot resist, such as a Dalmatian bitch puppy, so it is back to training classes again. I am continuing with Carriage Driving for the Disabled and have additionally taken on the role of Regional Representative for the south-east so have to visit all the groups regularly. Instead of competing at carriage driving I am now judging locally and learning how the timing mechanism works. I have also just enjoyed a splendid holiday in Ethiopia exploring rock churches and the wildlife, and scrambling up cliffs whilst ignoring the large drops off them.

Deirdre Waud (Ward) held a reunion last March for various old Holfords with **Miss Valerie Byrom-Taylor** (ex-housemistress) in anticipation of her eightieth birthday later in the year. It was a full volume affair with many reminiscences, some of which were a revelation on both sides of the teacher/pupil divide! Those who came were **Clare Jordan (Gore-Langton)**, **Diana Graham (Gantlett)**, **Sally Birnage (Clifford)**, sister **Gilly Stuart Smith (Ward)**, **Davina Instone (Vetch)**, **Carol Brook (Kynnersley)** and **Lorraine Clemie (Gibbs)**, who spent most of the day travelling to and from Yorkshire. They all felt much older (and wiser?) but Valerie B-T was just as enthusiastic as ever and looked just the same.

Deirdre was also in touch with **Judy McGill** and **Anne Millman**, who, as it turns out, lives only ten minutes from her, and she tried to contact **Jane Binney** with no success. **Deborah Martyr** was unable to come either but, when she was next over from Indonesia they had a very jolly lunch in London later in the year with Claud and Davina. Deborah had been awarded an MBE in 2015 for her services to wildlife. Deirdre says any other news is boring by comparison but she is still playing tennis, skiing and sailing in spite of one new knee and the other one needing attention.

Section 41 (1971)
Section Representative:
Jennifer Cope

Nicky Currie (Penley) I am working part time for our local agricultural college, Easton and Otley, as an agricultural apprenticeship ambassador, and as a link between the college and the farming industry. This has the wonderful advantage of four-day weekends whilst still challenging the 'little grey cells'. Our daughter Alex married Cedric Genot in May 2015 in Uley, Gloucestershire, where my brother kindly lent us his house. Alex has lived in France for some years now where she teaches English. Our granddaughter Mathilda was born last May, narrowly missing her parent's first wedding anniversary. Mathilda's christening took place on a proper summer's weekend in August here in sunny Suffolk. I continued to be involved in Suffolk, Norfolk and Hadleigh Agricultural Societies as well as some work to help those retiring from the military into second careers. My personal achievement in 2016 was to gain second prize for my tomatoes in the village produce show - well, you should see the competition!

Mandy Mac I have now retired and am enjoying travelling. I went to Kyrgystan, China, Pakistan and Vietnam last year and am off to the Comoros islands in April. We are so lucky to have been born when we were.

Karen Broomhead (Fielding) spends a lot of time in France renovating a villa in the sun. When in UK, she does fence-judging at various horse trials and supports her son Simon Grieve in his eventing career.

Section 40 (1970)
Section Representative:
Jennifer Cope

June Barrow Green I moved house last year which, due to the fact that I managed to fall in love with a house that had been hardly touched for a hundred-and-fifty years, turned out to be rather more time-consuming than I had intended. I am still in Islington but now have more space for my books and am less likely to be found buried underneath a pile of them! I am still at the Open University and am now also a Visiting Professor at the LSE. I do quite a bit for external organisations and last year had fun being on the External Advisory Panel for the fantastic new Mathematics Gallery at the Science Museum in London. I'm still running cross-country, half marathons and marathons, although I rely rather more on sports massage than I used to! I keep promising myself to get back into tennis but the house took up too much time last year. I see **Lee Twist (Beanland)**, **Shan Rigby (Jones)** and **Clare Jordan (Gore Langton)** regularly, and last week my sister **Belinda** and I had a great evening at a gig of John Coghlan's Quo where we caught up with **Gillie Coghlan (West)** who was in tremendous form and looking wonderfully glam!

Jane Lazurus (Kindersley) We continue to be busy like everyone else and still in our house after thirty years. Nick is married to a lovely Anglo-American lady and they have two boys, one just two weeks old! Their life is full on, and we are both enjoying being grandparents. They are not too far away in west London, while Benjamin and his wife, another lovely lady from Sweden, have just renovated a house in Shoreditch while continuing to be city-based for work. Rupert is now a working actor having completed three years at RADA. Bill is still working, but I have retired and am working as a volunteer in a state school and other organisations. I still cherish my WB friends: **Janie Odgers (Townsend)**, **Judith Barton (Evans)** and **Sarah Niven (Walford)**.

Barbie Matthews (Powell) We certainly have had an interesting year, with lots of highs and lows. We had a wonderful month in France in June and then when we got home, Peter was diagnosed with bowel cancer. He had an operation and we felt very fortunate as it was caught early and he did not need any further treatment. The day he was given that news I was informed that I had a malignant melanoma on my leg. In November I had this cut out and it required a deep cut, so more recovery time in our house over the autumn. We had booked a long and exciting trip in May to Hong Kong, Australia, New Zealand and America leaving on 5th January. Mid-

December we got the good news that we would be able to travel. We have just returned from over ten wonderful weeks, with six-and-a-half weeks exploring the south and north islands of New Zealand. We loved every day and have seen some wonderful places. We lived in Hong Kong forty-one years ago and I had not been back, so that was really interesting, and also Washington, where we lived twenty-five years ago.

Section 39 (1969)
Section Representative:
Liz Jubb (Grant)

Many of you will now know that very sadly, **Lissa Mills (Elliott)** passed away suddenly in January this year. She was in Sedgwick and then Beaufort. I have no further information.

Louise Dixon Has there ever been a moment in our lifetimes when politics invaded the essence of our day to day lives as much as now?

The tragedy of corruption and its accompanying ills - a failed education system, unattractive investment environment, a major shortfall in the much-needed low-cost housing stock, massive unemployment, poor healthcare - is that it's always the poorest in society who are the hardest hit.

There is a great deal of discussion in South Africa about the "decolonialisation" of education, history, society, business and even maths(!) How tragic it is that a magic wand can't be waved over history, like a sticking plaster, and for South Africa to be able to embrace the infrastructural, legal, constitutional, governmental, technological, industrial, mining, agricultural advantages and more, that made South Africa the powerhouse of sub-Saharan Africa, and to run with that ball to the advantage of all its citizens. That apartheid was horribly wrong is not for debate, but it's a double tragedy for those who suffered thereunder to destroy the legacy advantages that the country could offer to all.

We are fortunate to live in a leafy suburb of Johannesburg, where we are grateful every day for the wonderful climate at six thousand feet, for the cosmopolitan, multi-cultural environment, for the wide streets and wealth of glorious trees, and as we admire the view from our favourite cafe, which is the far point of our daily walk, we could be deceived into thinking that all is well.

Alas, the reality is that with youth unemployment at about forty per cent, with violence between MPs inside the debating chamber of Parliament and the council chambers of some of the major cities, with so-called students bringing the universities to a standstill with violent protests, with unrealistic wage demands and violent strikes, volcanic rumblings cannot be ignored.

The solution is not simple. Mass employment is a global problem, but in South Africa, as in America and the UK, citizens have the power of the ballot box and we must hope that they use that power wisely.

Noni Graham (Paton) I am not sure I have any very dramatic news. We are deliberately doing a little less B&B - I have taken the decision that I will not do any dinners this year, but the little self-cater Garden Studio will, I hope, work its socks off! It is a lot less work. Older son Rory has recently joined KPMG as a management consultant trainee in London and happily lives with his girlfriend. Younger son Neil is teaching English in Madrid and singer-songwriting when time allows. I am not in touch with anyone from my own year at WB but surprisingly have three old girls of various vintages living within a mile or two! I have joined a sports club since becoming an OAP and I do circuit training and play lots of tennis in an effort to keep my weight and general health in check. It's good fun, and I am amazed at the fitness of some of the other club members who are over seventy! I work my spaniels all winter on local shoots and am hoping my youngest one, Freya, will have a litter of puppies later this year.

Caroline Heaton-Watson (McKane) All good with us, we spend half our time in London (Battersea - we are very pleased with our move two years ago) and the other half divided between our three children who all live abroad. We do grandparent duty with our little three-year-old grandson and baby granddaughter. Not really a duty as we love it! I still enjoy my swimming, tennis and Nordic walking when I have the time. I was very sorry to hear about **Lissa Elliott**, a good friend in Sedgwick and Beaufort.

Heather Jenne I continue to play lots of music and do the allotment, but have finished music teaching and garden maintenance. Recent major excitements are the acquisition of a sackbut (early trombone) and moving the polytunnel. I still sing in a chamber choir, an eight-person group, and run a church choir. I play early music with friends – recorders, a dedicated crumhorn group, and other combinations of instruments – and have recently taken to playing in a folk-dance band (red plastic trombone). It's great being fully retired and able to lounge around in bed till past 7am!

Liz Jubb (Grant) Last May saw my sister **Pat** and I return to the Yorkshire Dales where we used to have a family cottage to spend a very enjoyable few days together reminiscing and celebrating her 70th (a memory seemed better than an unwanted gift!) Glorious weather was the icing on the cake. At the end of May we returned to Bude, for a week where we indulged in wonderful walks and plenty of good food. In June we spent ten days in Majorca where we were fortunate to be given the use of an apartment owned by close friends.

Thereafter things went downhill as I suffered increasing back pain through cysts trapping the spinal cord. These were removed in September, requiring fusion and insertion of plates but, more frustratingly, it meant I could do virtually nothing for six months. As I write, life is resuming its normal course, and I am trying to make up for all the diary commitments that were cancelled last year.

We have just returned from another week in Bude where we met up with **Clare Monro (Rust)** and her husband, Hugh, over a very enjoyable dinner. They were both in good form. Our house became very quiet last year when our cat, aged seventeen, had to be put to sleep, but we have now acquired a replacement from Cats Protection who certainly keeps us on our toes and is a real character - just what has been needed these last months! I continue with my village activities and photography, and Phil is heavily into singing with a major concert next month in Sherborne Abbey. Like others, I can't believe the years are going by so quickly and I try to keep down the weight, but it's a losing battle. (Well, we do live in Dorset where there are exceedingly good cream teas!)

The following have let me know they have no news this year: **Gill Carney-Smith (Smallman)**, **Kate McDowell**, **Kate Roberts** and **Liz Speller (Moore)**.

Jo Ledbetter (Salz) We have had a busy year in the gin business. Tarquin has branched out with some interesting new additions: the Sea Dog which is 57% proof, the Crocus using croci grown on the Roseland Peninsula and harvested by hand by dedicated growers, another Gin with baobab for the Eden Project, and the Tonquin using Tonka beans that taste of chocolate and sour cherries. Meanwhile, we are now grandparents to baby Felix, six months, who is still delighted every time we sing Hickory Dickory Dock. Elder son Duncan is still training in the West Country as an ophthalmologist and perfecting his cataract operations. The world still seems a much lesser place without Foxy and Angie but on we all go ... Brexit and all!

Denette Matthews (Skeil) I've had a busy family year. My son Jamie married Alexa last July, so we had all the fun of being involved in their wedding planning. They are now in the process of buying their first house and have a baby due mid-September. My daughter Jo has, after thirteen years given up her career in the super-yacht industry and come ashore to set up a kiteboarding school in the Western Sahara. As you can imagine life isn't boring. In the meantime we continue to sail in the summer and run a shoot in Suffolk in the winter months. We're making the most of being fit and healthy. Long may it last.

Lindsey Moffat (Thomas) Life here is not getting any quieter, what with horses, dogs, weather to deal with. We acquired a West Highland terrier puppy four months ago to add to our other two, and she has turned the house upside down. As cute as cute can be, which is just as well as otherwise we'd have left home! But seriously, she gets on very well with the other dogs.

My home-bred mare, now turning five, has been winning over the winter (dressage) which has given me immense pleasure and satisfaction. But best of all we recently celebrated the first birthday of our granddaughter Grace, who is a talking walking joy. Having lost our first grandchild, Hannah, to a devastating rare occurrence in utero very late in pregnancy, she so precious. They live next door so I see her every day. Her favourite words just now (forgive the indulgence) are do-do (dogs) and 'at (cat). She sees them all the time so it's not surprising. I am known as 'clip clop' - the noise the horses' hooves make, so that's me in my place.

I have been thinking of **Angie** and **Foxie** a lot recently. The lunch we had in London - they were just the same as always. We live on in the memories of our friends.

Clare Monro (Rust) We have seen Clare and Hugh twice in the last year, and she told me that she didn't really know what to put in the magazine! They are enjoying life in Bude with both of them heavily involved in local activities. I am hoping that on one of their visits to Kent to see their grandchild, they might break the journey with us!

Carolyn Monty (Tanner) The best thing was taking my boys (thirty and twenty-eight!) on holiday together for the first time since early teens last July. We went to the west coast of Portugal, and it was heaven. Then I was finally persuaded by Miles to ski again for a weekend in January. Haven't been for fifteen years, but the ski clothes still fit, and I guess with ten years' experience living in/around mountains in my twenties, no problem, and it was also heaven. Very happy bunny!

Jill Powell (Fawkes) I have been in touch with Jill over a possible visit, and she tells me that life is good with them. She is now into photography, using a 'half-way-house' camera (a bridge) so doesn't need to change lenses. For the last two years, she has done a project of taking a photo every day for the year, which was fun and sometimes challenging!

Angie Rose (Waite) I have been fine, except for pneumonia since November, which was tedious, and have been left with tremor in my hands. I have tried to start riding again, but the muscles are not as willing as the mind! I have a fourth grandchild due in July, a girl I believe, so that's exciting, my son Dominic's first.

I'm still involved with Beards the jewellers as chairman. My son, Alex, has great and imminent plans to extend the business to a shop in Mayfair. We have had an office in London for the last four years, so this is the next progression.

Ruth Stark (Worrall) I am enjoying my technical retirement! Still living in Edinburgh. Professionally I am still working and have continued in the past year to enjoy the honour of being the Global President of the International Federation of Social Workers. We now have over three million social workers in membership in a hundred-and-twenty-four countries. A lot of the work is done from my virtual office by Skype and email, but I have managed a few trips in the last year to USA, China, Japan, South Korea, Finland, Austria, Greece and Switzerland, where we have a tiny office! This year it will be Zambia, Zimbabwe, Kenya and Iceland. My husband, John, has been on some of the trips but says the long hauls are getting too much! It seems a big leap from the daily round of social work in the UK to speaking at the UN and talking with political leaders around the world - not quite on my radar when I was at Westonbirt all those years ago! The children are now in their thirties, and, with three grandchildren, life continues to be busy.

Jane Williams (Daniel) We had a family wedding in beautiful County Kerry in August. Our son Justin who works for Investec in Cork, married Emer Walsh, a solicitor from Fermoy, County Cork. The little church beside the lakes of Killarney was a wonderful setting for the service. It was quite a contrast being mother-of-the-groom this time - no responsibilities at all except for the wedding cake!

Most of the past year seems to have been taken up with sorting Johnny's late brother's house in Dublin. We have become quite expert in hand-searching at the Registry of Deeds for title deeds, etc. Although some parts of the search have been frustrating, the history of the property is very interesting. We were delighted that the Architectural Archive of Ireland took all the architectural plans drawn by Jeremy over more than forty years. A group of friends are hoping to underwrite the re-publishing of Jeremy's gazetteer on Victorian Architecture in his memory.

Daughter Ciara has been living on Edwards Air Base outside Los Angeles since last June, when her husband Alex was transferred for further training by the RAF. Grandsons Feargus and Lachlan (four and eighteen months) have been having a great time, skiing and beaches both within easy reach. They will return to Marlborough this coming June, just in time for Feargus to start 'big' school!

Welsh pony number five, Shanny was purchased in June - a Section C this time - bought in Scotland but bred in Wales! She had a baptism of fire last summer, going straight into jumping competitions. A well-deserved winter break has now ended, and she has just gone back to join her ten-year-old rider for more excitements. We hope that she will compete at the Dublin Horse Show this year.

A surprisingly early spring has meant that the garden looks very colourful and is beginning to look a little more mature since we moved in seven years ago. We continue to be active in our local GIY group in Graiguenamanagh, primarily growing your own vegetables, but the evenings always end up with a glass of wine and a good chat!

I continue to work part-time at Goresbridge Sales for the sport horse sales. It certainly keeps my brain cells alive when I am asked to 'spot' on the rostrum!

Was so sorry to hear of the passing of some of the most talented in our year. It's odd how one still feels relatively young (except for the creaking bones) but are now heading into retirement plans. A sobering thought indeed.

Section 38 (1968)
Section Representative:
Chris Shaw (Morris)

A lot of us seem to have become busier as we have become older, not only because of our involvement with our growing families, but also with travelling for work and for leisure, as well as developing hobbies and pursuing new interests. It seems to me that sixty is definitely the new forty, and by extension eighty must be the new sixty! It's good to have all your news and to know that we seem to be leading active and interesting lives.

Penny Bysshe (Osborn) has also been on her travels and will soon be undertaking granny duties: We returned recently from a fabulous ten week trip to Malaysia, New Zealand and Australia. I am still catching up and getting back into the routine of dance teaching and running tea dances. I see **Alison Gauld (Taylor)** regularly. My first grandchild Oliver was born last May and is a great delight. Julia took a year off work and is going back to full-time work when she returns from a month in Argentina with her husband Steve and baby Ollie. Steve is researching fifty high-end hotels in Argentina for his travel business for the indecently rich. Such a hard job but someone has to do it! We will have regular babysitting duties from June onwards, but only for one day a month.

I am very involved with Vibez Dance Studios in Woodley near Reading and teach ballroom, Latin and sequence dance classes and private lessons. Peter and I run tea dances there on a regular basis. It is good fun, but the admin required to keep it all running smoothly is time-consuming and tedious. The couple who own the studios are barely thirty and all their staff except me are very young. Working with young people is great fun and certainly keeps me on my toes! They are kind enough to say they benefit from the wisdom of my great age and from my business experience.

I started ballroom and Latin dancing eleven years ago and since then have achieved awards level as a lady. Three years ago I decided I wanted to become a dance teacher and learnt how to dance as a man as well. I have been studying for my professional dance examinations and will take my first one at the beginning of July this year. Over the past eleven years I have competed successfully in a great number of dance competitions as an amateur both in this country and abroad. I am now going to concentrate on teaching dancing and will no longer compete. It was wonderful to do well in my last pro-am competition at Blackpool in January this year and to come away with three firsts, two for ballroom and one for Latin!

Deborah Dorrance King (Dorrance) We are all well and kept busy. The boys are all settled: Charles as an architect in New York; Harry graduated from LSE with a Masters in African Development and will join the Civil Service Fast Track either as a generalist, or the FCO – there are pros and cons to both; and Ralf, the youngest, finally went to university at twenty-three. I have been away quite a lot this year, firstly, to our son's graduation in New York, after which we went up into The Berkshires. The lakes, mountains and forests are wonderful. August saw me in South Darfur with a medical NGO, an interesting experience, followed by a trip to a southern town on the Blue Nile in February, bodyguard not required. David and I had a great time in November in Chicago, a town I had always wanted to see overdosing on architecture and meeting up with old friends. Otherwise I keep busy as a churchwarden.

Julia Douglas (Neath) There has been a heavy wedding focus over the past year – our eldest daughter Laura was married on New Year's Eve, and our youngest Mia is due to tie the knot on July 29th of this year. The event is scheduled to take place in a large Kentish barn, and I am already having sleepless nights about how to decorate the place!

That only leaves our son Bruce to make up his mind, but I think that may be a long way off! He is still living in Brazil where he was working as a freelance journalist in Rio de Janeiro, but has now moved to Brasilia, having secured a job with Bloombergs news agency. We managed to make two visits out there in May and December respectively and no doubt we will make more in the year to come.

By far our favourite holiday, though, was a touring holiday in New Zealand at the start of last year, where we were enchanted by the beautiful scenery and the remoteness of the place.

Most recently we have been to Costa Rica, another country with a huge amount of biodiversity. Closer to home, last July we had a very enjoyable visit to see Martin and **Chris Shaw** in their charming house in Tetbury, and inevitably took a trip down memory lane by visiting the Arboretum whose visitor centre is very grand now, as well as the grounds of Westonbirt, with our spouses.

Back home in Sevenoaks, I have started working for the Witness Service at the local magistrates' court, basically taking care of people who have been called in to give evidence, a role which can be interesting, frustrating and depressing at times. I punctuate this with "granny duty" on Fridays for three-year-old Inky and eight-year-old Timo at their house in Oxted, with trips to London and keeping fit by playing tennis and walking. On the whole life is pretty busy, and I can hardly believe how quickly time goes by! Apart from Chris Shaw I still keep in close touch with **Judy Kramer (Nettleton)** who until very recently used to come over to England from Spain to visit her elderly mother.

Jane Fisher (Binney) I now have four grandchildren, two in London and two in Myanmar, and our youngest, Susannah, is expecting her first in May. I am still working as a therapist, specialising in trauma, and we continue to travel for work far more than we anticipated at this stage of our lives. My focus has been mainly in Zimbabwe where I have been working for a long time, and recently writing a book bringing together western and traditional perspectives on mental health. As I write, we are both in Beirut for a month, working with Syrian exiles and others who can still travel in and out from Damascus and other cities. Later in the year we will be back in Cambodia. I still love it and am fascinated by all the stories and people we meet, but when I get back to Oxford, I wish I were staying put and never travelling for work again!

Diana Gale (Forwood) had visited Westonbirt last year for the AGM and sent me some photos, mainly of people from the few years above us, so it was fun trying to match faces to names. Di reports that they had a very good meal! She says the highlights of her year included becoming chairman of the tennis club committee.

It is only a small club with two courts and a playing membership of just over thirty, but we recently became affiliated to the LTA and, despite my natural Luddite tendencies, I have been trying to update the club. We now have an email address, a club website and accident report forms and did a health and safety inspection before our Grand Open Day. One new member is ex-WB first team player **Annabel Kerr (Johnston)**, who recently moved with her daughter and family to just round the corner. New house, new baby is the saying and, sure enough, Anna's third grandchild, a second girl, was born in January.

I had my usual Christmas letter from **Hilary Hughes (Moore)**. She, too, has a new granddaughter who arrived last June. Hilary is still teaching at a university in Brisbane. She had some fantastic travel opportunities in 2016 with her research projects including trips to Amsterdam, Vancouver, Denver and Wellington.

I enjoyed last year's Westonbirt AGM and am glad the State Rooms are being so well looked after, restored by the Holford Trust, and those bell boards were fantastic. I was very pleased to have attended Miss Newton's memorial service. It was lovely, especially the duet by present pupils. **Katharine Hill**'s eulogy was excellent, and the music was good.

Alison Gauld (Taylor) Jim and I have been busy over the last few years with our elderly parents. My father is the only one left now and is in the Royal Masonic Home in Bury St Edmunds where I visit him every two or three weeks on a three-hundred-mile round trip. My brother and I are in the throes of selling his house near Burnham Market on the north Norfolk coast. Jim and I are both enjoying his early retirement, and our time is taken up with bowls and bridge. We spent a restorative three weeks in Paphos in November where we were able to play bridge and bowls. I keep in touch with **Sue Bottell (Rigley)** and **Penny Bysshe** who are very dear friends.

We enjoyed a trip to Dublin for Sue's son Tim's wedding last August in a beautiful setting at a hotel on the beach of a sandy bay. My own son Kristian is the Base Captain of Newcastle Airport for Jet2, and is extremely busy with his job.

The four grandchildren are now fourteen, twelve, eleven, and ten, so growing up fast. Barnaby is at Reading Blue Coat School, and he is showing signs of being good at drawing and looking forward to the cricket season.

Tilly loves her sports and is at St George's School, Windsor Castle. She is tall for her year, like me.

Jamie and Lucy in Newcastle are both at the same secondary school, where Jamie can be in mainstream yet in the special needs department for his learning. He still has great difficulty speaking, reading and writing but he loves cycling, cars and motor bikes, and is a most endearing, kind and helpful boy. I continue with my voluntary work as a hospital driver and with the church, taking home communion to those who request it. I am trying not to take on anything else, apart from cooking nice food for all who visit.

Chris Shaw (Morris) Thank you to everyone for sending news of your many and varied activities. I'm inclined to agree with Ruth when she asks how did we all get so old? 2018 will unbelievably mark fifty years since we left Westonbirt, and I have canvassed you all about organising a reunion (doesn't seem long since our fortieth!) to be arranged around the Westonbirt AGM in October 2018. The feedback has been positive, and I will get back to everyone nearer the time with concrete suggestions.

Like Julia, Di and Ruth, who have all visited Westonbirt in the past year, we are occasional visitors from our home in Tetbury. We have attended an Open Day complete with tour of the building, walked in the grounds, and been to antiques fairs. I agree with Ruth that much has deteriorated over the past fifty years and, without realising or, probably, appreciating it, the gardens were at their most glorious in the sixties, tended by large teams of gardeners. However, we live in different times and the pressures of running an independent boarding school combined with the maintenance of such a large and historically important estate and grounds must be horrendous. The restoration of the Library and some of the main rooms has been done sympathetically and well. The clearing of the grounds, the restoration of the Camellia House and ongoing work on the Italian Gardens have begun. However, most of this work depends on the fundraising and expert research done by the Holford Trust. The school, like so many, is also tapping into commercial revenue streams such as venue hire for weddings, events, conferences and open days. I commend people to look at the websites and to visit the school and gardens – it's interesting to see the gradual turnaround, but it seems painfully slow.

Having sorted out our various house moves, Martin and I are finally able to enjoy "retirement". We spend about a third of our time at our townhouse in Tetbury, which a relative recently commented seems like an upmarket B&B. I took it as a compliment, but it's also fairly true!

We have five grown-up children (with grown-up problems!) and four grandchildren under the age of seven. That involves quite a few visits either to or from them during the course of the year.

We also have friends and relations from home and abroad who are easily seduced by the thought of a few days' stay in the Cotswolds. We have a smaller but picture-perfect cottage in a village in North Yorkshire which enables us to keep up our Yorkshire connections from the last fifty years or so. One day we may have to opt for one or the other home, but for now we are happy to sit on the fence – or, more literally, keep driving up and down the motorway. Our reward for running open house over the last year was to give ourselves breaks in Cyprus and South Africa. I find the warmth very good for arthritis!

Diana Sichel (Ferguson) became a granny this year: We are being really chicken about the house moving decisions but lots of uncertainty about work, health etc. The important thing seems to be busy. I have been helping Buzz get back to work. Martha is now six months old. Very hard for this generation in their mortgage traps. Anyway, it has been delightful playing babies – all my paediatrics got remembered. **Janet Johnson (Plowright)** is in the same situation, but we haven't swapped pics yet. I saw **Jane Fisher (Binney)** before she went to Lebanon for a month.

Ruth Watson (Genden) has also visited the Westonbirt area.
Our restaurant with rooms, the Crown and Castle in Orford, Suffolk, continues to take up much of my time, although I now work a three day week. That still means about thirty hours a week, including one evening in the restaurant, so it's not negligible. And when you think the French consider thirty-five hours to be a full working week. Which brings me neatly on to Brexit. The decision to leave the EU caused me, and continues to cause me, genuine grief. Weirdly, on the day of the referendum I was visiting Highgrove with a friend. I hadn't realised the implication of the date when I'd booked the tickets. We had a great, slightly irreverent, guide, and Prince Charles's devotion to horticulture and nature is very evident, but I still think the gardens would benefit from a proper designer!

After Highgrove, we drove to Westonbirt, the first time I'd been back in nearly fifty years. I know there are fundraising efforts in place to resurrect the gardens, but I was really shocked at the derelict condition of the paths and stonework, and the paucity of planting. I remember everything being immaculate, but obviously it took a large team of gardeners, and they cost money. There were many changes, not all for the better architecturally, and I came away thinking that we had lived through a golden era in terms of amenity. Of course, that is probably tempered by the activities and coursework being far more diverse, and the opportunities wider ranging.

As usual, I have been in charge of major refurbishment at the C&C including new windows and flooring in the garden rooms, swanky bathrooms in four other rooms and a comprehensive update to the restaurant. A new outside eating area, protected from the onshore winds by glass screens and from the sun by a huge five-by-seven metre umbrella, should be in operation this summer. We won a coveted award in Sawday's 2017 guide for Fabulous Food and, indeed, I think this is the best kitchen we have ever had.

At home we have just planted a two-hundred-metre hedge, and we bought the cottage on the edge of our land when the previous owner died just before Christmas. We are currently refurbishing it with a view to letting it out, preferably for a long-term rental as Suffolk, particularly the coast, is being ruined by holiday lets. It's time the council emulated Devon and Cornwall where they have woken up to the harm caused when more than half of a village is unoccupied for eight months of the year. Schools, shops, garages etc can't survive on part-time residents.

Our two fox terriers are in good health, although Annie is now thirteen, and her son Teddy will be nine this year. We are very lucky in having someone who housesits when we go on holiday, this year to Corsica for the first time, and then Turin and Venice in late autumn. We normally only go in mid-winter, when it's empty, but are celebrating a friend's seventieth, which obviously determines the timing. How the hell did we all get so old?

Section 37 (1967)
Section Representative:
Jenifer Davidson (Moir)

Sultana Al-Quaiti (Rashid) Friends Of Hadhramaut (*www.hadhramaut.co.uk*) is celebrating its twentieth anniversary in Paris on May 13th, and my daughter Fatima is expecting her second child in May. I enjoyed being at the AGM last year and catching up with **Lucy** and **Moi**.

Alison Boxley (Muir) No news but she has asked me to mention that our year has a get-together every year with around fifteen to twenty people. Sometimes a lunch, sometimes a weekend and occasionally longer (she is thinking of the breaks we had at Sarah's). We try to vary the format - different date/different venue so as to be as inclusive as possible. Last year we hired a Youth Hostel in Street, Somerset and it was such a success we are doing another Hostel in the Welsh Borders this year.

Anne Collings (Watson) 2016 wasn't good. My husband, John, was diagnosed with myeloma two days before we were due to travel to India for a three-week holiday in January. He responded well to chemo and was pronounced in remission, so it was decided that the best chance of a lengthy remission was for him to undergo an auto-graft (a stem cell transplant). The process was very gruelling, but he bounced back quite quickly once he was out of hospital and after attending a Myeloma UK support meeting he decided to sign up for the London to Paris bike ride in May this year.

His training was going really well, he was a keen cyclist, but at Christmas he suffered a very sudden and aggressive relapse, which caused pneumonia and complete kidney failure. He died on December 30th two days before what would have been our forty-sixth wedding anniversary.

My eldest children Freya and James are doing the bike ride in his memory. Freya is a haematology consultant specialising in myeloma, which made her father's diagnosis even more difficult to come to terms with. The full story can be seen on the Myeloma UK London to Paris web pages.

My youngest daughter, Bryony, has a six-week-old baby, so even though she wanted to do the ride as well, it was too impractical with such a young baby. We have all been fundraising, and Bryony organised a Family Fun Day in our local village with bouncy castles, baby animals, horse-and-carriage rides as well as cream teas and many fete stalls, which raised a magnificent sum of nearly £2,000 for Myeloma UK.

We have all been keeping very busy and hope that 2017 will be a more positive year.

Jenifer Davidson (Moir) I seem to be as busy as ever, still working part-time and doing various voluntary jobs. I very much enjoyed the reunion at Street last May and am looking forward to seeing everyone in July.

Karen is actually in a different section to me (36). The same applies to some of the people who were at the reunion – from memory and looking at the photos the following were there. From Section 37: **Eileen McGregor (Bond)**, **Hilary Davis (Stone)**, **Alison Boxley (Muir)**, **Sue Pasfield (Ross)**, **Venessa Pugh**, **Jane Savage (Fowler)** and **Cas Boddam-Whetham (Burkitt)**. From Section 36: **Karen Olsen**, **Alison Parry (Sturdy Morton)** and **Lucy Fisher (Sadleir)**. Query - not members of the Association; **Ruth Precious (Richards)**, **Christine McLaren**, **Rosemary Evans** and **Daphne Sanders**. Not sure I know what to say about any of them except that no-one seems to have changed much over the years and that it was good to catch up again.

You may have more news from the Section 36 rep.

We send our condolences to Anne on the death of her husband.

Section 36 (1966)
Section Representative:
Julia Braggins (Cock)

Thanks so much to everyone who has written in. And wonderful to see so many of our generation, celebrating fifty years since we left school, at the reunion at Westonbirt last October.

Moi Beveridge (Adamson) News v v boring this year. Was going to move back to the smoke but think too old and lacking in courage so downsizing in Somerset instead. Thought of moving YUK but shall advance upon bottle for solace. Had to have dog (staffi) put down and decided not to replace - freedom and all that - but couldn't take it as first time in my life no animal at all so just found another staffi christened Humphrey! Anyway not a lot else (no history of my good works) and shall just continue pootling along. How lucky I am. Hope to attend reunion and thanks again for our fiftieth. Frightening!

Julia Braggins (Cock) I really loved seeing so many of our year at WB, some of whom I hadn't seen for fifty years. From the inside one feels nothing much has changed, but our outsides told a different story! Really appreciated all the efforts everyone had made to give us a good day, and the beautiful surroundings (as they have always been – though less appreciated by me in earlier years, as we trudged off in our grey macs on wet afternoons). Thanks so much to **Sandy Marshall (Hellawell)** for putting us up, and to her husband Desmond for taking Peter off to a (more manly) rugby match.

On the personal side, a trip to Australia, our first ever holiday of that sort of length and distance, was the highlight of last year for me. Otherwise, I am happily engaged in the same activities as last year, much involved with our grandchildren, everyone well, thank goodness, and continuing to love living in this beautiful corner of Kent.

Judy Chesterman (Clarke) It's been a year of change in the Chesterman family. My cousin's lovely wife, Lynda, died rather suddenly in May, which was a great shock to the whole family. Our second granddaughter, Isabel Rose, was born on 29th July and christened on March 5th, thus giving us all something to celebrate. Sophia (granddaughter number one) started school in September, seeming impossibly young. She has taken to it like a duck to water, however.

In November I decided to retire; it's a wrench, but you have to bite the bullet sometime, and this seemed as good a time as any, particularly with the uncertainty of a date for my hip replacement operation hanging over me. At the moment it is scheduled for 4th April (at last); I do hope they don't change it!

In early December, Arthur and I went to Vienna to celebrate forty years together since we met there while making a film for the BBC. It was wonderful to be back there together, and in addition I found myself at the opera sitting next to someone I haven't seen since I was at RCM. What a small world it is! Emma is doing well in her variety of new careers, and is very happy in her house. We are delighted to be shot of the builders at last and are having fun recreating the garden.

Sarah Ferguson At the time of writing I am in Wanaka, Otago, NZ. For the four months I spend away I prefer it here rather than Northland for the social life, biking, hiking and paddle boarding. I'll be back in Dorset at the end of March for another season at the hotel taking care of the grounds. We now have an Ashtanga Yoga centre in Studland, and I am learning the Primary Series. It is energetic, but thanks to years of Iyengar Yoga I am strong enough and keen to defy old age and the inevitable pull of gravity.

Sandy Marshall (Hellawell) Many thanks for organising our gathering at WB in the autumn. I think Gloucester probably won the prize for the most attendees, and **Sue Westcott** for name recall. It was a pity we could not go up to the Dorchester dormitories, but the now former Holford ones were a revelation – I had never seen these before!

The following weekend our son got married on an organic farm in Somerset. They then spent three months travelling in South America – they have sympathetic employers. Pictures on Facebook meant being able to track their progress, very different from my VSO years when posted letters were really the only way to reassure the parents one was still in one piece (and telegrams from them when they felt letters were getting too sparse).

Earlier in the year we took our campervan to Orkney in June for the music festival there - wonderful to come out of a late evening concert and find it still light. I also managed to sing in Slovenia and Sardinia, and join the BBC National Chorus of Wales in Tippett's Child of our Time, one of the Albert Hall proms (televised, but fortunately cameras were trained on the front row glamour) in July.

Looking at last year's news to try to avoid repeating myself too much, I found **Di Knapp's** mention of the glass harp concert at Westonbirt. I too remember this: it would have been one of two concerts a term, one compulsory, one voluntary. Many were by musicians who later became famous – John Ogden, April Cantelo, who perched on a stool and talked to us directly, as I remember. We used to wonder at the age of the audience, who seemed so elderly then - less so now of course, but I think we were lucky to have been exposed to such excellence.

Karen Olsen This past year has seen me with new eyes after two successful cataract operations. I now have prescription lens implants in both eyes so no longer need contact lenses which I wore for many years. It is great to get back to night-driving again which I had had to give up until my eyes were fixed.

On the family front, we enjoyed a lovely wedding in Richmond followed by the reception in Petersham for my niece last July. For my sister, **JackieWoodgate (Olsen)**, to organise a wedding in the same year as moving house for the first time in twenty-four years was quite stressful. It was made more difficult as they were downsizing from a large farmhouse, but there is very little property around to downsize to. Initially she and her husband and a lot of furniture came to me until they managed, in the interim, to buy a flat, which needed total renovation. They moved in for all of a few days until the electrician arrived to do a complete rewire, creating so much dust and mess that they were back to lodge with me again. This went on over several months last year, as the bathroom was re-plumbed, the kitchen refitted, and so on. I have now got my home back but the garage is still full of furniture which is not mine! Eventually they hope to find a smaller house but there is nothing on the market yet.

It was great to catch up with some of my year at a reunion in Street in Somerset last summer and also to see several members of Sections 35 and 36 at the Association's Reunion Day in October.

Alison Hope Parry (Sturdy Morton) I have continued to catch up with the world and my bucket list. Amazing two week road trip through British Columbia in August - so many WOW moments from the mountain views, ice age glaciers, impromptu swim in a mountain lake, bears walking along the other side of a freezing rushing river where I was dipping my toes, wild deer etc, to seeing a bear just walking along the main road beside the car.

In January, a friend suggested going to Australia for February. We visited Melbourne, Adelaide, Alice Springs, Port Douglas, Brisbane (Kakadu tame compared with Daintree) and Sydney... a mad amount of traveling and we only scratched the surface!

I loved Alice Springs, Uluru (amazing and different colours at any time of day) and the outback experience round there; visiting some "stations," talking with the people who live miles from anywhere, the flying doctor service, and sitting in on the school of the air. Kangaroo Island was full of wow wildlife moments - kangaroos hopping around fields just like rabbits in the cool of the early morning and early evening, koalas asleep high up in trees raising a head to glance down at us and best of all that David Attenborough moment when a tired mother seal came out of the sea and called her pup. Baby much further down the beach, hadn't had any milk for a couple of days; head comes up at mother's call and replies, rushing to a happy reunion and the teat. Nature is Extraordinary!

It has been a year of great change. My son and daughter in law moved to New York, a decision made pre-Brexit and Trump! My daughter and family returned to France and the Pyrenees from Guadeloupe, exchanging Christmas on the beach to one over log fires! My granddaughter attends the village school – twelve children from five to eleven taught by one teacher who sticks to the French curriculum but then takes the lot on adventures from grape harvesting and making their own grape juice in a vineyard to a couple of days skiing! It's lovely to be able to talk in real time and see them all more frequently.

It was wonderful that so many of us were at the reunion in Street: such a fun time. Thank you so much for organising us, Ali. Am looking forward to similar reunion this year!

Tilly Patricia Roberts I'm acclimatized to living in a three-bedroom apartment in Santiago. It's so easy closing the door and disappearing off to my cottage without having to worry about watering the garden or checking to see if the house is safe.

I continue to work in a small rural school in the Cajon Del Maipo valley. I train Project Trust volunteers in August each year to work teaching English there. The volunteers are two British girls in their gap year. They do a wonderful job once they've got over culture shock and can communicate in Spanish!

It was a pleasure to return to WB reunion lunch last year and to meet up with Section 35-38 leavers. **Marilyn Jones (Bird)** very kindly had me to stay and drove me there. It was fun seeing **Jules** (head girl) with the WB present head. Evidently they both shared similar problems!

Section 35 (1965)
Section Representative:
Marilyn Jones (Bird)

*My thanks to **Philippa Dutton (Thompson)** who, sadly, has been the only contributor of section 35 news this year!*

Philippa Dutton (Thompson) I am totally adjusted to semi-retirement. Life is full with seeing friends, making music and spending quality time with my husband Dickie.

I was honoured to be accepted as a Member of the Worshipful Company of Musicians last July, with grateful thanks to Petronella Burnett-Brown (past Master) who was one of my nominees. Since then I have become a Freeman of the City of London, enjoy many events promoted by the Livery company, and am now involved as a volunteer with their Outreach programme taking young prize-winning musicians into primary schools. Having left The Bach Choir after 39 years rehearsing every Monday, I enjoy singing with a number of small choirs who perform on four or five rehearsals. I also continue to play chamber music with a couple of friends, sadly not as much as I would like.

For the third year running I have been invited to join the Royal Garden Party Office at Buckingham Palace where, with four other like-minded ladies between February and May, I help to prepare the 40,000 invitations. As an Honorary member of four of the Royal Warrant Holders 'local' associations, I continue to enjoy various functions promoted by them and to keep up with Warrant holding friends.

Holidays were cycling down the Moselle Valley in August, our favourite haunt in Turkey in September and Capetown in January.

I have seen **Janet El-Rayess (Welsford)** and **Caroline Revitt** this year and was pleased to attend Miss Newton's Memorial Service with **Eleanor Fountaine (Bateman)** in October.

Marilyn Jones (Bird) As for myself, a very busy life with eight grandchildren, four of which have been living with us since last July with their mother, our daughter Amy. Managed lots of travel, however, a month in India a month in Java/Australia/Fiji, and several shorter trips.

Delighted to have been visited by my old friend, **Tilly Roberts**, from Chile, who stayed with me last October . We attended the school reunion ; it was lovely to meet up with so many old friends after 40 years . Hope it's not another 40 before we do it again!

Section 34 (1964)
Section Representative:
Julia Popham (Bishop)

Ann Beattie (Buckland) I am guilty of taking advantage of the lovely spring sunshine we have had and getting out in our small garden. We decided last autumn, having seen one that a friend has, to buy a Veg Trug for the patio so that we could grow a few veg and herbs. John and I put it together in the autumn and then it was empty over the winter. This pleased our cat Suki who decided it was the best place to sit in and watch the birds. Last week, with a strong east wind blowing on a sunny day, we filled it with endless bags of compost, covered it with the empty bags to stop it blowing away. Now she thinks it's an even better place to sit. That will have to change when I start planting.

Last Autumn we made our first trip to Norfolk, spending a week self-catering in Holt. We were well placed to visit various places along the north Norfolk coast from Titchwell to Sheringham. Wonderful beaches and big skies, good birdwatching for us fair weather birders! We liked Holt and may go back that way later this year.

Carol Brawn(Topham) My youngest, Emma, is now 42 and is a GP in Exeter with two girls. Lisa is at Torquay Grammar and is a great artist and loves sport, and Chloe, aged nine, is a keen gymnast. Victoria continues as principal oboeist at Orchestra of the Swan in Stratford and Birmingham, married to Jeremy chief trainer pilot at DHL, with Isabella, aged twelve,with an amazing voice, just done Grade 8 singing and awaiting results, with great violin and oboe and drama! Will, aged ten, is doing Grade 5 French Horn and Grade 3 piano, He is also black belt karate and drama. We cannot keep up with them all. Husband Bill is down to one to two days a week advising, more than operating, around the country in paediatric cardiac surgery.

Our eldest, James, is in Shanghai at the Face Arts Institute, teaching the piano from ages three to seventeen to amazingly talented kids, and doing concertos and auditioning for top music institutes in the USA etc. His girls are 23 and 21. Olivia is end of fourth year at Oxford Brooks doing sports car engineering having had the third year working for Bentley and hoping to do post-grad back there, while Ophelia is in middle of arts and interior design. I am doing the garden and supporting them all and the two labradors!

Clare Carter (Binney) I have been concentrating on getting properly mobile again after the back problems of the previous year, plenty of short walks and swimming, all of which were very good for me and improved things a lot. My only trips were one to Oxford to see my sister, **Jane**, and a lovely weekend in southern Ireland with the choir, a wonderful social weekend during which we gave a concert in a lovely little church. I hit a big birthday in the summer and the family ignored all my pleas to forget it, for which I'm really glad, as we had a wonderful celebration here in mid-August. Both the children and families/partners came, plus **Jane** and some of her family. We had a weekend of celebration with everyone but Ben's family came for two weeks (no sense in any shorter from Japan), which was great. It was the first time Ben's wife had been here, his son too, and the first time I'd seen my grandson for three years, so I was in heaven.

The second half of the year has been less exciting as my cancer relapsed in the autumn. I had some chemo before Christmas but it didn't achieve much so I'm now on a different regime, not much fun but just has to be got through. Ben came over again in February and Helen will be here at Easter. I also have lots of help and support from my U3A friends, and I still manage to contribute a bit by acting as activities coordinator.

Mary Cave (Rawlence) (*I received news about Mary from* **Elizabeth Ells (Rawlence)** *who is Mary Cave's older sister*:) Mary is incredibly cheerful in the face of adversity. Her MS is increasingly debilitating but despite physical constraints she still enjoys her regular French group, reading novels which I might not tackle even in English. She and Christopher still live in their three-storey house in South Croydon despite the many stairs. Sadly other sister, **Emily**, died very recently after having suffered from Parkinson's for many years.

June Cohen (Kefford) As the next big zero birthday looms, as it does for many of us this year, I have done a little reminiscing and much family history research. The former was prompted by a little book called *"Terms and Conditions"* by Ysenda Maxtone Graham and published by the intriguing sounding company, Slightly Foxed. It draws on the memories and stories of many women who attended girls' boarding schools, between the years 1939 and 1979. There are sadly only three or four Westonbirt references, but it is, nonetheless, a book full of reminiscences that will certainly ring bells and jog memories and either bring tears of regret, sadness, or laughter to most.

My family research has dug up a fascinating and deeply unexpected rags to riches story of my maternal grandmother, about whom I knew nothing a year ago, all mostly thanks to the wonderful facility of ancestry online.

As for current life, no massive changes there. Husband, children and grandchildren all thankfully well and happy and fun to be with. I am very lucky. Our eldest granddaughter, having just turned seventeen, is learning to drive, but I think causing her father rather less stress than he did to me at a similar stage in his life! I am thankful that, at the moment, gardening and tennis still give me more pleasure than physical aches and pains, but sometimes only just! School governing, church work and my choir manage to comfortably prevent the onset any incipient boredom.

Charlotte Essex (Humpidge) It has been a year tinged with joy and sadness. Our autistic niece died suddenly in April last year, followed five days later by our great-niece, aged nine, in a ghastly riding accident. But joy as well with the wedding of our godson and my seventieth birthday celebration with family and friends, which was a wonderful day to remember. Andrew and Jo have sold the lease in the café, which had been an uphill struggle. Zofia is very happy in her first year at primary school and enjoys coming here to stay. Jonathan and Gail returned to Thailand to see her parents again and continue to take in overseas students. Catherine is enjoying a challenging job with the NHS at the Maudsley Hospital as PA to the Chief Executor Officer. We continue to exhibit at antique fairs, and, what with gardening and general cottage maintenance, there's little time for retirement! But we have booked a holiday to Corfu in May, which we are looking forward to.

Susan Fisher (Barritt) Not much to report. We are still enjoying retirement on the south coast, where we live in a flat looking out to sea. We also have a flat in London, so have the best of both worlds. My husband is finishing off the dissertation for his Masters, whilst I am involved at my church with, amongst other things, Toddler Club and Messy Church. We sometimes look after our ten-year-old grandson who seems to enjoy spending time with us by the beach or in London.

Anne Grocock It's my impression that the years do get shorter as we grow older, and it seems no time at all since I wrote this note last year. I am still working as a non-executive director for Oxford Health NHS Trust and battling with the financial situation in the NHS. Our greatest expenditure is on staff, and it is becoming increasingly difficult both to recruit and retain staff. Brexit does not seem to have made it any easier as in the health service and also in universities employees come from all over the world.

From a personal point of view, I have just celebrated my 70th birthday, and, like a number of contemporaries, I am trying to have a special event every month for most of the year! I have not seen many WBs this year but I met up with **Chris Bryan** both last summer and recently in February when she was over from the US. Bill and I are slowing down and not going away much, though we did have another wonderful holiday in Ireland last year. We also see his children and grandchildren regularly and were delighted to learn that one granddaughter is representing England at rounders! I hope to catch up a bit more with WB next year when I think I shall finally retire!

Claire Marshall Same old, same old - but perhaps one shouldn't say that at our advanced age! I'm happy and healthy and keeping out of mischief. Excellent trip to Iceland last year, highly recommended though thronging with tourists. Still chairing OrKidstra's Board, this year celebrating our tenth anniversary with now more than 525 students (www.orkidstra.ca if you care to see what the fuss is about). 2017 is also Canada's 150th Anniversary with myriad special events, from death-defying downhill speed-skating to mechanical monsters forty feet high prowling the streets.

I joined a new choir with a broad repertoire and a chance to sing in many languages. Such a thrill to be challenged by music. Recently performed Dvorak's *Stabat Mater* with a second choir. So grateful that my voice is still there.

I am in the midst of compiling life stories of cousins, aunts and uncles from my Mother's side (twenty-four lives, 1915-2017). A similar exercise for my Father's side (twenty-two lives, 1904-2016) proved a great success with insights, photos and new-found closeness across continents. Big families make it intriguing! If anyone is interested, I could share writing guidelines to get you going.

Rosemary O'Malley (Matthews) I have no work now of any sort (finished with the voluntary commitments with the Magistrate's Advisory Committee), but my husband Brendan is still very active in church life and takes services every week, so still the same 'wife-responsibilities' there: clearing church, churchyard bins and brambles, typing things up and generally being there! I still garden, walk the two whippets twice a day, paint (whatever has inspired me on my walks), and play the flute. Then in the summer months, there is all the outdoor maintenance that has to be done. I keep fit, but the old arthritis has made me rather odd to watch when I'm doing jobs (so Brendan tells me!) Brendan's health is not so good, but that's life. Best thing we can do is be aware it's not for ever and value what we have when we have it. So we are fine.

Julia Popham (Bishop) My nagging to my Section this year seems to have worked and we have had a bumper response! Many, many thanks to you all - very much appreciated.

Nigel and I enjoyed a week's holiday on Lake Garda in September last year, having travelled there by train which was fairly eventful with riots in Paris, and long delays at several European stations, but we saw magnificent scenery whilst travelling through Switzerland. We also had a few days staying in Tetbury in June celebrating our fortieth Wedding Anniversary. We especially enjoyed our tour of the Arboretum which was looking magnificent, and I was reminded of cycling into Tetbury from school and gorging at The Close, where I believe we could eat as many cakes as we wanted for two and sixpence! (I think it closed down fairly shortly afterwards!) *(Ed: No, The Close Hotel is still open and thriving, though probably a bit different these days!)*

Just before Christmas our thirty-five-year-old daughter, Clare, heard she has been awarded a place on a heavily oversubscribed government-funded two-year scheme leading to a Masters in Social Work. She will do her training based in Newham and will be living in Woolwich. Our son and daughter in law and their two children (aged five and three) live in nearby Earlsfield, and I look after James and Eliza every week, but they will be moving to near Chippenham in a year or so. Nigel and I continue to enjoy playing golf and to be involved in local politics and our local church, where I am about to become a churchwarden again (for the second time in twenty years!) We continue to have guests over Wimbledon Tennis for bed and breakfast. We are looking forward to celebrating our joint seventieth birthdays in June and to a number of short breaks during the course of the year.

I would like to conclude by extending, somewhat belatedly, very warm congratulations to **Pippa Dutton** who, in November 2014, was invested by Her Majesty the Queen as a Member of The Royal Victorian Order for her services to the Royal Warrant Holders. Pippa had worked at the Royal Warrant Holders for seventeen years.

Joyce Seaman (Carnegie*)* My husband, Tom, and I press on with our day jobs and try and have fun in our spare time. We have visited our son, Alastair, who is now working in New York and loving it. I am hoping to celebrate seventy years with two Westonbirt friends in the summer. It is a slightly daunting thought!

I have been working on a group of mid-twentieth-century Japanese prints at the Ashmolean Museum and had a very enlightening trip to Japan in November to see the various museums dedicated to some of the artists. All the artists have now died, and many have museums dedicated to their work, often in the towns where they were born or grew up. It took me all over the place.

Many long but enjoyable train journeys to get to remote towns and villages were involved, but the rewards at the end were tremendous. In sharp contrast to those using Southern Trains at the moment, you can set your watch by the timetable, both departure and arrival. Should there be a delay of perhaps only three minutes, there are apologetic announcements over the tannoy system. All trains are spotless, and on the bullet trains regular food trolleys come by with tempting local fare as the train crosses the countryside. Speaking on a mobile telephone is only done in the corridor between the carriages. What a contrast to British trains!

In early November the autumn leaves are turning and in the temple gardens, in particular, the maples are spectacular. Scarlet or brilliant yellow leaves contrast with the austerity of stone and gravel, each branch having been carefully considered and clipped to give maximum impact. The effect is breathtaking. We lived in Japan in the 1980s and even though the pound now only buys you a third of what it used to, a hearty bowl of noodles is still more or less the same price as it was then. I do recommend Japan to anyone who has not already visited. It is endlessly fascinating, and you never quite know what you might see around the next corner. It is also a reassuringly safe and easy place to get around, even with no knowledge of Japanese, for almost everyone is willing to help.

Jo Wilson (Forcey) I am in South Africa at the moment where I come for three months over the English winter but return with the swallows in April! It's been a busy year going backwards and forwards to SA as I still have the farmhouse here with about fifty acres. My son has a business in Johannesburg, he is married to an English girl and they have a boy of three and a girl of two. Both my daughters live in London where the elder one, Tembe, has three daughters - number one at Benenden, number two going in September and the third hopefully going in two years. I went down to Grandparents' Day and stayed with **Anthea Shipley (Franklin-Adams)** who lives near the school and bumped into **Jessamy Reynolds (Smith)** who also has a granddaughter at Benenden. Since I have returned to the UK I have caught up with **Liz Graley (Constance), Jane Simpson (Witt)** and **Eleanor Fountaine (Bateman)** which has been great fun. I was also at our place in Spain twice last year so feel this year I should be less peripatetic!

Section 33 (1963)
Section Representative:
Helen Faircliff (Wienholt)

Anita Armstrong Now established in flat with two dellies (or delhis?) so come and visit Mallorca. Big swimming pool too.

Prue Bishop (Taylor) 2016 was a year when we managed to get away almost every month to a different part of western Europe. We had not been to Vienna since 1972 and were impressed by the care that had been taken to keep alive Austrian traditions in architecture, music and painting. Of course, we had to re-experience the special magic of Viennese opera and ballet.

Then, in pursuit of my ongoing historical research work, we went to Heidelberg in Germany and all the way up the Neckar Valley to Heilbronn, partly even by bicycle. Next we investigated in detail the entire route over the famous Mont Cenis Alpine Pass between Chambéry in France and Italy's Turin, meeting some really nice people along the way. Some of this took us back to the amazing days of Charlemagne, around the year 800.

Next we were up near Cambridge digging out nineteenth-century sketches of Swiss scenes in the Wisbech and Fenland Museum, and we squeezed in a memorable day in Norwich too. I also continued with Swiss locations as subjects for my on-going Sculptural Watercolours. As this is now a registered trademark and the British Library archive my web site, I feel that at last I'm making some public progress, and so I'm looking forward immensely to taking this side of my activities ever onwards!

Suz Burroughs (Bradbury) Just playing tennis, croquet and bridge, and continuing to work in the garden and growing my veg.

Sue Coveney (Hyman) I have closed my West End office and although handling some PR, am very enthusiastically gardening at Kew which seems like paradise. I am trying to remember all the Latin I learnt at Westonbirt to understand every plant/tree name.

I keep in touch with **Helen Faircliff**, **Denise Bittolo (Porter)**, **Caroline Henderson (Beloe)**, **Julia Tingle**, **Anita Dudley (Armstrong)** and **Alannah Rylands (Watson Hall)**; the latter must be the most brilliant and knowledgeable gardener in Cumbria.

We have two wonderful and lively granddaughters and they live very near.

Liz Davies (Edwards) I am still living in Weybridge with all the family within easy reach. We try to see the grandchildren every week and at four and seven they give us enormous pleasure. We have booked a week together on the South Coast in August as a belated celebration of my seventieth. Much of my time is involved with my local church and also my hobby of family history.

Mary Gillham (Woodrow) We had a super four days in Dresden last year. It is an amazing city. Most of our "holidays" are in Cornwall helping with the grandchildren. Our grandson with Costello syndrome is doing really well and loves his village primary school where he is beginning to learn and develop socially.

Casha McNab (Robertson) We have been busy, away on a trip to India and working hard on plans to downsize into a smaller, modern, warm house which we will build in our garden, provided that we get planning permission.
Really not much news. Just busy with our family, grandchildren and travelling quite a lot while we are still hale (so?) and hearty. Keeping fit as much as possible. Am still playing league tennis so have to work harder at it every year. Not seen anyone from WB.

Sandie Russell (Morris) Well, we are still on this planet, which is a positive as so many of our dear friends seem to have left this mortal coil. Both of us are well and hale and hearty. No new hips, knees etc needed, though Stewart did have cataracts removed successfully last year. He can now see much more clearly, not always to my benefit as he keeps asking who the "old woman" is that lives with him!
Our main news is that Jamie, our youngest, and his family emigrated to New Zealand in August. We miss them very much as we saw a great deal of the three grandchildren, but they have landed on their feet. They both have very good jobs, a lovely house and all three children love their respective schools. I am quite tied up this year with Fife DFAS (part of NADFAS) till June, but we hope to get out to see them next January/February.
Bridge still continues, but I have given up club presidency this year. A friend and I had a lovely break walking in Malham in September. An area we were not familiar with, but loved it."

Jane Simpson (Witt) We have recently returned from a month in South Africa, a long overdue visit to see John's old school friends and the few remaining relatives he still has out there. We haven't been for eleven years, and we saw a tremendous difference. Cape Town was glorious, Durban not so glorious. Unfortunately John had been in hospital for a month at the end of last year with meningoencephalitis, which was very nasty, so a good bout of sunshine was much needed. We had our youngest grandchild's baptism at our tiny village church here in October, which was lovely.

Otherwise we have been busy still doing things to the house such as new windows throughout and a new front door, so we are pretty well hermetically sealed now! A new greenhouse is due to arrive at the beginning of March, which I am very excited about, and hopefully it will lead to some good crops this summer. Otherwise still involved in village activities and our four grandchildren.

Kate Thompson (Richards) I am still a governor of the Music Therapy Charity and we are appointing a new chairman. The charity's remit involves funding research to provide an evidence base. This is an interesting example of how music therapy works: www.bbc.co.uk/news/magazine-39435646.

Music also continues to feature with our grandson, Jimmy, who is now in his third year as a chorister at Westminster Abbey. This year already he has sung at services attended by the Queen, and the Pope during a visit to Rome!

Julia Tingle Am still involved with the hotel where I used to work, as I was asked to go back in the summer of 2016 to cover an emergency staff gap for two months, and am now teaching the EU hotel staff English once a week. Current attendees are Polish, Romanian and Hungarian. Previously Spanish, Italian and French also attended, but have now moved on to other jobs.

Am now in my ninth year of being a guardian to Japanese schoolchildren, but thinking of giving it up as half-terms can stretch interminably up to fourteen days, and helping with exam revision is not easy when English is the second language!

Being on the parish council for the last two years has kept me aware of planning nightmares in the locality, as well as being involved with CPRE Sussex, who do a sterling job of protecting rural environments.

Otherwise, this year marks a quarter of a century of living happily in the same home where I recently invested in foam insulation in the loft to try to stop heating the lane outside, and hope for reduced electricity bills as a result.

I'm hoping to meet up with **Jessamy Reynolds (Smith)** and her husband when they come to Glyndebourne, and also lunch with **Liz Davies (Edwards)**, and a mutual friend from HK days, sometime in the summer, hopefully combined with a visit to an NGS garden nearby.

Helen Wienholt (Faircliff) A busy and eventful year as my mother died in April last year aged 101, and the rest of the year was been spent dashing up and down the motorway sorting out her papers, selling the house etc. It has taken months just to sort the paperwork. Moral to us all: don't hoard!

I have bought a tiny Barefoot caravan whom I have named Petit Escargot. She is small, but nicely formed, and I am planning to have six weeks away in the summer in the south of France just to chill out. So the start of many nice adventures I hope.

My son, Simon is getting married in May to his long-time girlfriend. They are doing all the planning so am just going to turn up on the day suitably clad. They have just bought a cottage in Kingston, so it is lovely to have him living nearby.

I have seen **Sue Hyman, Susie Iliffe, Suz Bradbury, Sue Burns, Mandy Smith** and **Lin Maiden** (over from South Africa) during the year, and it is always good to catch up with everybody's news."

Rosemary Wolfe (Callard) Last year we went to India, Bhutan, Iceland and New York. In February 2017 we went to St Lucia, Guadeloupe and Dominica, and enjoyed exploring three different islands.

I have seen **Wendy Taylor**, **Helen Bianchi**, **Juliet Peel** and **Gay Durston** over the last year, and keep in touch with **Gill Jordan**.

I am still teaching music at home in Derbyshire, and trying to cut down. I play badminton, sing in a choir, and walk with a local U3A group, and we run a local music Club.

Section 32 (1962)
Section Representative:
Sarah Rundle (Milner)

Once again, thank you so much to all who have replied this year. It is so good to hear from everyone even if they feel their news is 'boring', and I apologise for the nagging!

Helen Bianchi (Fairbrother) News is always difficult as cannot imagine anything very riveting to say. Still working as a practice pharmacist in a GP surgery. We have a new grandson, born last June, so amazing to learn what ideas have changed since last grandchild nineteen years ago.

No holidays to report, except our annual visit to Norfolk which we really enjoy. On the way back, I joined **Gay Woodley (Durston)** and party to see *L'Elisir d'Amour* at Nevill Holt which was excellent. Then in July Gay and I spent an action-packed couple of days at Buxton Festival - an opera, two literary talks and a concert - where we met **Ro Wolfe (Callard)** and then enjoyed lunch together. Great to hear news from **Gill Jordan (Atkinson)** and wish that we could somehow all meet up - so many shared memories.

I have started piano lessons again - concentrates the mind and am really enjoying them. Paul has just had a back operation which seems to have been successful. He is so grateful to be able to walk properly again.

Cannot believe that WB news is on Amazon!

Denise Bittolo (Porter) Renovation of our building took more than six months, during which time it seemed to be one endless day of banging and drilling. Finally in December, it was finished, and we are now gradually getting back to normal. The garden suffered the worst, with stones and cement literally everywhere. To aid this we have had a bout of three months of terribly cold weather which managed to kill the few remaining plants not destroyed by the builders. We are going to have a busy time re-doing the garden once spring arrives. Hopefully it will not be long because the blossom is already on the fruit trees.

My second son has now opened his own construction company and is up in Rome all week renovating villas. It means our babysitting duties with his two children are longer but somehow we manage to cope. Next year should be a little easier as both children will be at school, Luca at elementary and Simone at nursery.

We will be flying over to Tenerife in August to see our eldest son, Riccardo, who is now settled over there with his family. We will have not seen our grandson Manuael for two years.

Healthwise both Gino and I are doing well. I had a small tumor removed from my leg earlier this year and have had two ops on my hand, in fact as I am writing this I have one hand bandaged up and am due to have the stitches removed today. Thank goodness these are all minor things one can cope with.

As most of us did I celebrated my seventieth birthday in September with a wonderful luncheon. Family and close friends enjoyed a typical Italian Sunday lunch which ended at 6 o'clock in the evening!

Elizabeth Bryant Having stayed with friends in Germany before the referendum, when we all decided it would probably be Remain, I was faced with incredulous friends in Copenhagen in July who couldn't believe the result. By the time I went to Naples and Pompeii in October, we were definitely feeling the effect of the falling pound. Pompeii and Herculaneum were wonderful, quite different from what I'd expected, and the weather was bright but cool, ideal for wandering round.

I had a few days in London in December, seeing old friends and visiting old haunts. I went to hear The Sixteen in Temple Church, re-visited the Hogarths in the Soane and went for the first time to the Foundling Museum.

Otherwise, I am still enjoying Bradford-on-Avon. **Mary Hudson** and **Phil Shaw (Northcroft)** have both been to stay. I go regularly to the Wiltshire Music Centre where there are wonderful concerts, Academy of St Martin in the Fields and the Orchestra of the Age of Enlightenment. Unfortunately I had a hacking cough so had to give back my ticket to the Alison Balsom which was sold out.

Just planning this year's holidays. Bologna and Ravenna next, Sicily and the Isles of Scilly later in the year. I've always wanted to see where Admiral Sir Cloudesley Shovell ran his ships onto the rocks. (Wonderful name - and Sir Manley Power is buried in Bath Abbey.

Carolyn Henson (Iliffe) I have been living here in North Yorkshire for over six years and I love it here. I am twenty miles from the coast and twenty miles from York. People often come and stay and visit the whole area, which includes the Wolds. I am semi-retired, still practising as a psychotherapist, and licensed with the Diocese of York with what is called Permission to Officiate. It means that I can take services in this parish, and in other parishes if asked, and I am very glad to do this.

I have been making a lovely garden here since I moved in, and I am still gardening and enjoying this very much. My garden is now almost completely planted. The blossom trees have opened up this week, and spring seems truly to be here.

My family is growing well! I now have three great-grandchildren. My sisters are very well and come to stay here at Christmas and New Year. Sister **Jennifer**, who is married to an American, is living in the USA but about to move to England this summer. She and John are selling their home in Georgia and moving to a new house very near me in Malton. They will be in England again in May and then will eventually move to live here in about July. I am looking forward to this, and so are they. **Susie** is still living in London. She now has two grandchildren and is a really hands-on grandma, and very good at it. We three sisters are now all in our seventies. I must say my sisters do not look it at all, but I am the oldest and having to come to terms with getting older. Thankfully, I and my sisters are all feeling fit and active.

Jyotipakshini/Erica Rigg (Harding) I know I'm late for the News but this is just to say I'm still alive and kicking. Kicking limited at present as I'm heading towards a hip replacement.

Mary Hudson Apart from Antigua, last year was a horrible year. However, so far so good this year. Medical problems are being sorted, both for me and good friends (some ex WB), so it can only get better?

Sarah Rundle (Milner) I have to agree with those who have described Brexit as a tragedy. I worry about the future for our grandchildren, especially the family who live in France. I just hope that common sense will prevail.

Life here in Cornwall is much the same and goes very fast! Robin's health continues to be of concern. He has now been diagnosed with Non-Hodgkin's Lymphoma as well as Parkinson's. We have found the medical staff at Treliske Hospital in Truro to be wonderful. I will not dwell on the disaster that is the administration!

We have had no priest in our local church for nearly a year now. The wheels of the Church of England grind very slowly with a huge amount of work expected from volunteers. I continue to sing with our local choir and love it - huge fun, and we often sing anthems that I learned in the choir at WB. I will always thank WB for my love of classical music and singing. One of the highlights of my year is The Sixteen's Choral Pilgrimage in Truro Cathedral.

Phillida Shaw (Northcroft) Having completed thirty-three years promoting and advising on historic and contemporary stained glass on behalf of my City Livery Company, the Worshipful Company of Glaziers, I am looking forward to the opportunity to travel more widely with my husband, who retires this year. Having been a glass engraver for forty years, I am now looking for new creative challenges!

Deborah Soper Last year I did trail back and forth a bit across the Channel, twice to my now four-year-old granddaughter in Shrewsbury (a fairly complicated journey from Guernsey). She has already started school and seems to be thriving on it.

My sister and I caught up with **Sue** and Robert **Whitfield (Bottomley)** at their beautiful house near Westonbirt.

We went to Bardolino, Lake Garda in May, and to Whitby later on and I visited my niece and family in Virginia shortly before the dreaded election. She lives in a beautiful, pretty rural area with a couple of elderly horses, chickens, ducks and dogs, and her family, of course!

I had the big birthday party in May which spilled over into my garden and was really good fun. A friend brought a sumptuous three-layered cake he had made decorated with fresh berries and cream, and my son brought loads of wine and food.

The rest of my time is divided between gardening, life drawing, pottery, enjoying nice meals with friends and family, going to an exercise class twice a week, reading and being lazy (last but not least!) - pretty near perfect really. I feel really blessed.

Sue Whitfield (Bottomley) 2016 certainly had its horrors, and (for me, at least) the sad Brexit business is a continuing tragedy.

On the brighter side, we acquired a new grandchild (number 10), the first child of our son, meaning we have not had the normal involvement of the baby's mother's parental backup, but simply have the pleasure of regular visits from son and daughter-in-law and dear little Charlie, who very sensibly lives half way between his two sets of grandparents, with a journey of twenty-five minutes in each direction.

Meanwhile, I will soon be retiring as a governor at Westonbirt after what will be nine years. I am still involved with a benevolent charity which was originally set up for governesses in Victorian times, adjusted as times changed to include schoolmistresses in need, and from April 2017 will be re-formed in a more modern form of charity and renamed the Teaching Staff Trust (formerly 'SGBI'), and will give grants to men and women who have worked, or are working, as teachers or in teaching support roles in schools and are in dire financial straits. By being reformed in this way, it will be able to help more people more easily, as well as stay in touch with those who have been beneficiaries in the past under its earlier arrangements.

Together with family activities and the busy life in our hidden corner of the Cotswolds, life is full and enjoyable. I am hoping to have more time soon to do more writing. I so enjoy reading various things from the generations above me that I feel a duty to write a bit for my grandchildren about my grandparents and my own childhood.

Gay Woodley (Durston) Gradually been slowing down this year due to a bad back, and now both my hips need replacing, also had to have a hernia operation in March. Kept at the yoga to try and stave off the inevitable, but June is now booked for number one.

We had a great holiday with Verity and co in Tuscany in August, after spending two weeks on our own in the smaller hill towns. We were by the Seine on our way to Giverny on the day of the referendum and couldn't believe the result; we were given some aggressive looks the next day. We revisited the Menerbes area in September finishing up in Nimes on the day of a bull fight - no parking anywhere, but wonderful atmosphere in the streets with paella to eat and a display of Camargue horses.

I bumped into **Priscilla Llewelyn (Rickard)** Section 31, at The Grange prep school in Monmouth; both our grandsons were in *Noye's Flude*. My granddaughter is very keen on lacrosse, she certainly didn't get that from me. She plays at Westonbirt every year.

I am still enjoying our NADFAS and my opera class, though Wagner is still not number one for me! I watch as many of the streamed performances of opera and ballet as possible, they are wonderful.

Section 31 (1961)
Section Representative:
Priscilla Llewelyn (Rickard)

I am so pleased to have received these news updates, all of which are of interest to the rest of us.

Vanessa Cook (Hall) I am still growing plants and opening the garden, we have a cafe now and have opened for the National Garden Scheme (NGS) for thirty years. Just makes me feel old!

I have three grandchildren at various universities, and now I also have two tiny great-grandchildren, doesn't time fly?

I would love to see anyone, and I am sad that I am too busy to go to the wonderful Garden Festival at Westonbirt at the end of March.

Sue Garden (Baroness Garden of Frognal) (Button) Both at home and abroad, we are certainly living in interesting times. Life continues to be busy for us Liberal Democrats in the Lords. I have duties on the Woolsack, speaking and chairing engagements and a focus on higher and further education, skills and apprenticeships. I have had breaks in Florence, Nice, Devon and Japan.

My daughter Alex has been appointed chief executive of Hampshire Hospitals, while Antonia continues as a primary teacher. The four grandchildren are all now teenagers and great company. Outside the Lords, activities and interests continue as before, counting the blessings of wonderful family and friends.

Priscilla Llewelyn (Rickard) I am very lucky. I have a good family life (nine grandchildren now) and an ever-developing business which keeps me happily busy. In fact I fear that over the years I have spent far too much time on the care home, but it has proved to be a fascinating subject. People are coming in about ten years older now than when we started thirty years ago, and living twice as long but with much more demanding care needs. What a conundrum! Anyway, I have booked my room for the future in twenty years' time.

I'm also refurbishing a cottage in the village, which keep its old façade but not much else. It's a very intriguing project and fills all those spare hours that can be found.

Singing, first encountered at WB sixty years ago with **Miss Naylor**, has proved an uplifting interest, and bridge (not learnt in our days at WB) a brilliant social attribute.

I went on my first cruise at Christmas – got absolutely hooked – and I'm going on another one soon to study Greek and Roman history through the Mediterranean, so must get cracking and get this news sent off before I go.

Jane Merritt (Wilkinson) It has been another great year with visits to family in the US and in Denmark. I joined Michael, Monica, Cecilia and Marcus in Soller in Majorca last August for a week, and then spent ten days with them in Denmark. It was a great time. Keith could not join us because of Rotary commitments, but we are booked to visit the family in Denmark in August this year.

Cecilia has spent a month in Ghana, and two months in Tanzania on a student teaching program. This has been a great learning experience for her living among the poor. She climbed Mount Kilimanjaro with a group of students and spent a week in Zanzibar. Keith and I met up with Michael in Washington, DC for a weekend. He was on his way to a conference in Seattle. It was fun to visit the museums and see the sights of Washington again.

Keith and I are still very much involved with Prison Ministry and the Episcopal Church. After fourteen years of weekly broadcasts on the local TV station, I have stopped the Called to Serve interviews. Now, Keith and I have a little more time to get away to the beach in the off season and take advantage of the quiet, empty beaches for runs. I am still singing in the choir at church and love being challenged by our Music Director who practically grew up in Liverpool Cathedral. The sacred music he chooses is wonderful. We are both blessed with good health and energy. If anyone plans a trip to NC, please let me know - it would be great to be in touch!

Sue Patchett (Greenwood) Well, things move on in the usual way, despite Brexit, Trump and any other unmentionable things we can think of. Australia is limping along, and although we have been lucky over the past few years, there is a quiet air of apprehension everywhere.

We sold our farm three years ago, which was very sad, and the whole family miss it, but we had fourteen years there during which time we saw floods, droughts and drenching rains, as you would expect, but also plenty of Aussie bush (kangaroos, wallabies, echidnas, wild pig) and lots of wonderful birds, never mind the cattle and sheep work – it's a wonderful life.

I am fully retired now from Patchetts Pies which I started over thirty years ago. Dan, my son, has taken the reins, which he did when I contracted leukaemia a while back. The cancer returned three years ago, but I managed to see it off again so am back in Sydney, busy with youngest grandchild (5) who has just started school. My son has two children, Charlotte (13) and Oliver (11). My grandchildren are, of course, totally delightful!

I am in touch with **Rosie Heygate** and **Felicity Ashwell** intermittently. Fash comes out to Sydney to see her daughter, so I see a bit more of her, which is lovely. Other than that, life passes in a very pleasant way – retirement has lots to recommend it, I find.

Gillian Wynes (Ross Goobey) It was lovely seeing my son and his family when they were over here from America in June, and to see how much the grandchildren had grown in the six months since I had last seen them. My son and granddaughter came back last October for my younger daughter's fiftieth birthday party, and it was lovely to go out to dinner with them. Otherwise life jogs on at Adlington House (Independent Living with Care), we have quite a varied social life, film, speakers and quizzes.

Section 30 (1960)
Section Representative:
Jane Reid (Bottomley)

Bodhiniya (Ann Udal), Penelope Cowell (Bowring), Phoebe Field (Northcroft), Jenny Greatwood (Bawtree), Anna Ingledew (Willliams), Joan Madonko (Scott), Jane Palestini (Macfadyen), Juliet Peel (de Galleani), Elizabeth Reisz, Carolyn Reynolds (Mathison), Sallie Sullivan (Sanderson), Barbara Workman (May) had been in touch during the last year. Sadly, **Ingrid Divett (Jackson)** *died September 2016.*

Ann Beard (Harverson) Nothing exciting to say! I keep myself busy, enjoy our holidays and relish every moment with our four grandchildren and play crown green bowls when weather improves! I have been in touch with Penny Bowring on Facebook which was good.

Dinah Delchambre (Middleton, not a member) emailed that she was now almost half bionic, as have a replacement knee, two hips, one thumb and one toe! However, with a springer and a 'sprocket' spaniel, have had to walk, and am about to take up yoga which have not practised since my twenties.

Have just (early March) spent a week in Northern Cyprus, with a group interested in exploring the amazing ancient sites with which Cyprus abounds. Having been fairly ignorant about the long-term history of the island, am now extremely well informed. The ancient sites were amazing, well worth putting up with the heavy sales pitch over carpets, jewelry and leather goods. The Turkish Cypriots are very laid back and once away from tourist spots, so willing to please. If anyone goes there however, don't get Euros, but Turkish lira, you'll find everything much cheaper this way."

Janet Kingston (Oakeley) had, as usual, spent most of February in Australia, enjoying being looked after, and spoilt by our eldest daughter in her home in Melbourne. With so many visits behind us, we know our way around both in the city and the surrounding areas almost as well as at home. This year, instead of returning mid-March, we had left in January as I had an operation scheduled on the Ides of March for a total shoulder replacement which has proved to be quite a painful experience but at least is now behind me as I work hard at recovery. Not all those hours of violin playing at Westonbirt could prevent attack by arthritis!

Our youngest daughter, now a Major in the AGC, is about to commence her new posting at Larkhill, which is about as close to Stonehenge as she could possibly get, following her early fondness of archaeology. Currently feeling quite elderly especially as it's nigh on sixty years since I took my first O Level!

FelicityMacdonald (Northcote) *had, on the whole, not found 2016 to be a good year.* I had a whole series of minor ailments, nothing of major import but trying and restrictive. Domestically, my house, like me, is getting old and subjected me to an endless string of repairs and renewals, ranging from nearly every lightbulb in the house to the complete overhaul of my particularly complicated heating system, which took a frustratingly long time. Plenty of other things as well - life has not been dull.

Trying though all these matters were (and some still are as I write), nothing came near the heartbreak of losing my beloved little dog, who died last autumn. Muffin may have been 'only a dog' but I have been a childless widow for twenty years, and for the past fifteen of them he was my constant companion who shared my home and went everywhere with me. No great drama about his end, no apparent pain or distress he just lost his 'bounce' and simply faded away over a couple of months. He was very special and I miss him.

But 2016 wasn't all bad and, to end on a very happy note, the highlight of the year was my eldest great nephew's engagement to his delightful Emma, of whom we are all very fond. The family are very pleased. Rob and Emma have been together for eight years now and are a lovely young couple. I am particularly happy about it as they have bought a house about a quarter of mile from me and will be near neighbours. We hope the wedding will be next year. All the best to you all.

Carol Mullin (Rostron) emailed that she was living happily on the edge of Dartmoor, near a little grandson and able to be involved with his care; she was also still doing some illustration work.

Roma Part (Thorpe) replied to the News Request; she had no special news this year.

Jane Reid (Bottomley) got as far as September last year, getting rid of something for each day, but then the impetus faded. Her list shows progress, or lack of it – she was running about two months behind when she wrote. Meanwhile, a bout of cellulitis in the summer led to a number of health professionals advising her to lounge about with her leg up. She took to this so over-enthusiastically that in mid-February she discovered that the strength of her leg muscles had reduced to near-useless for getting up from chairs, going up and down stairs, turning over in bed, and therefore sleeping properly. So she took to daily walks (with Nordic trekking poles – very useful in Storm Doris to keep her on the pavement) and got advice from the local physiotherapy clinic who gave exercises to strengthen the muscles and lubricate the joints while protecting the arthritic knees. Six to twelve weeks to see any results, they said. She hopes that with that low level of encouragement, she can keep at it better than she did the disposal of clutter. Use it or lose it, folks! (Or, for clutter: lose it or use it!) Her daughter-in-law was in the process of acquiring Irish nationality for herself and the grandchildren.

Rosemary Somers (Fuchs-Marx) Being fundamentally European, Rosemary had applied for and received German citizenship, something she had never envisaged! Her children would put in their own applications.

Extra double glazing had been installed to mitigate noise and vibration during the demolition of Earls Court exhibition hall at the end of their garden. Demolition complete, the biggest crane in the world, shipped in parts from Brazil, was being used to remove huge concrete beams before the creation of foundations above and around the District Line strong enough to support the replacement building (apartments). The disappearance of the exhibition hall gave welcome new sunshine at the back of the house; Rosemary and her husband were in no hurry for above-ground construction to commence, probably in 2018.

Rosemary's sister came from Canada to share in the celebrations for Tony's eightieth birthday. The sisters visited their old house in North London (Rosemary's home when at Westonbirt). Their mother had resisted painting the house; Rosemary was pleased to see it was just as it had been and, now being in a Conservation Area, would remain unpainted. They also visited the house in Dorking to which her sister had been evacuated when she arrived in England on the Kindertransport.

Tony was fit (CLL in remission, etc) and his tennis got better and better; both of them maintained a busy schedule of exercise, yoga, zumba and tennis.

Bridget Towle Still alive, though seventy-five approaching. When does life slow down? At present I am the Chair of the Council, the governing body, of the University of Leicester. Sometimes Miss Scott Smith's words reverberate, "Not degree calibre I'm afraid, Bridget". She was probably right, but she made me determined to go to university.

Section 29 (1959)
Section Representative:
Myrth Russell (Hudson)

Nonie Beckinsdale (Joan Hills) The most exciting news of 2016 is that both of us (Mike and I) had hip replacements, mine last January, his in June, both totally successful. Life was getting very limited and we dreaded having to walk any distance. I don't think we are in for the London marathon just yet, though.

Our children are getting positively middle-aged: son Tim, his wife Becca, and our son-in-law James all turn fifty this year. Jessie is still in Northamptonshire, painting when she can. Ros, our baby, started her journey to a nursing qualification and is working in Bristol at the Infirmary. Very hard work, but she seems to be loving it. Grandchildren are starting to leave school. Sam (20) went off to Canada last autumn to work at a ski resort in the Rockies. Ben (18) has a BBC traineeship, periods of study alternating with periods of work. Joe (16) is doing A Levels at Hereford and on the Welsh Junior Cyclocross squad. Barney (18) is in the last year of A Levels. Jake (15) and Anabelle (14) are still pre-exam stage. They all visit now and again and clean out the cupboards, fridge, freezer etc.

Mike, when he relinquished chairmanship of the local British Legion branch, thought he was in for a quiet life, but the present chairman seems to need an awful lot of back-up, and he finds himself a sort of unpaid consultant. I have managed to add MU branch leader to my portfolio. Not much hope of a quiet life there either!

Sue Bowden (Humpidge) All sad I'm afraid. Last April we lost Bonnie, a darling nine year old granddaughter, in a freak riding accident. Also our autistic and much-loved daughter Emma, all in the same week. Friends, particularly those from school days, have been terrific, but the ache will always be there.

Lin Coleman (Hutton) I'm still living in London, working part-time as a psychoanalytic psychotherapist with individuals and couples, a very interesting second career after many years in the world of EFL teaching and training. Apart from family, gardening and singing in a vocal jazz choir are my favourite pastimes, as well as visiting art galleries and exhibitions. I love meeting up with old friends from Westonbirt days (**Susan Humpidge**, **Libby Houston** and **Caroline Price**) and am looking forward to a larger reunion later in the year.

Angela Fenhalls If there is ever a desire for a London get-together, I would love to do it focused on Kew Gardens. I can offer two beds and get two people in free.

Leaving for Burma, I know that's its maiden name, on April 1. Obviously an ill-chosen date as husband Richard dreamt up a family trip as a fiftieth wedding anniversary celebration, and he had a minor heart op yesterday so cannot fly. It has been so successful he insists I should go, as he will be looked after by close friends. Another of the reasons was that grandchildren are reaching an age when family trips may not be so appealing, and it may be the last holiday we do all together. There are also only two of them so the logistics are not so daunting.

Kew Gardens continues to provide joy, knowledge and stimulation with the added plus of new friends. It can be daunting moving at our age, concerned about imposing upon children, but this has provided a new career for me. I mentioned Kate's Welsh farmhouse project before, and the house is now waterproof. I no longer have to stay in the caravan that she lived in for eighteen months.

Would love to share Kew Gardens with anyone who is in the area. The Hive, celebrating bees, will be open again from mid-April.

Libby Houston I'm still anywhere between 0° and 90°, paid or unpaid, as a botanist in the Avon Gorge, or sometimes as far as Lundy Island or Malham to battle invasive aliens (plants, not Martians) on cliffs. Amongst it all, I was quite taken aback to be filmed on ropes for BBC wildlife programme *Springwatch* - even more so to be presented with an Unsprung Hero award by Chris Packham!

Other odd events included speaking at a European Beat(nik) Studies conference two days after the referendum, and opening a convincing email and subjecting my computer to instant kidnap by ransomware. Or – kinder memories – a lovely summer day on Salisbury Plain with **Caroline Sturdy (Price)** and **Sue Bowden (Humpidge)**, in Caroline's gypsy wagon, and later introducing my urban grandchildren to Sue's many friendly animals.

We met up again, and with **Lin Coleman (Hutton)**, in just as bright November sun. I'm lucky to live a twenty-minute bike ride from my daughter and her three children; less lucky that my son and his almost grown-up family live in New Zealand. I'm also sporadically – or potentially – in touch with **Jennifer Scully (Parker)**, **Jennifer Cairns (Matthias)** and **Eileen Stewardson (Grosvenor)**.

Linda Morley (Northcroft) We didn't have any news printed last year but I expect you don't want much from 2015. I did go on a very interesting visit to Estonia with the European Union of Women in autumn 2015. The theme of our visit was migration, still a difficult subject. Members from seven EU countries were present.

Last May I helped to organise the AGM and international weekend of the Fan Circle International to Cheltenham. This proved to be quite popular with members from European countries and the United States. We visited local museums and country houses and were fortunately blessed by lovely spring weather.

Practically all of 2016 went in a flash as I tried to move house, which took nine months of torture! I am now safely established in a modern townhouse quite near where I lived before, more exercise, less housework, awaiting an imminent garden makeover.

Very sadly my son-in-law died unexpectedly last December, following a cancer operation. This has had obvious repercussions both for my daughter, who lives quite near, as well as myself. We hope for a brighter 2017. My two granddaughters, from my son Jeremy, are a joy to me, now aged eleven and seven.

Susanna Peake (Kleinwort) Susanna is going to join the OG. She says she lives a quiet life in the farmhouse she and her late husband had moved to recently, so has no other news this year.

Myrth Russell (Hudson) My second husband Andy and I have lived in Scotland for twenty-one years, hoping not to suffer another referendum. Three years ago, we moved sixteen miles from our peninsula home to Helensburgh, a small town in the Highlands, thirty-five miles west of Glasgow.

I still play the violin, mostly in string quartets. We give small charity concerts and play for parties and weddings, the latter always a great honour and often surprising and amusing.

My daughter Susannah, now 51, lives nearby with her ten-year-old daughter Kezia, who loves playing the clarsach. My son Patrick, with his wife and two children, lives in San Francisco, creating computer graphics for films, *Star Wars* et al. His son Ben is now at university in LA concentrating on drama lighting design.

I have liked being back in touch with other OGs. **Helen Brown (Todd)** wishes to be remembered, but could not send news this year.

Eileen Stewardson (Grosvenor) Both my children are living in Australia. At the moment (Sept 2016) I am recovering from shingles. I had a stroke about seven years ago which makes life seriously difficult).

Section 28 (1958)

Section Representative:
Sue Hicks (Harker)

I was very glad to hear from more of you again this year, and am still trying to get back to the numbers that Milada managed to produce.

Sheila Astbury (Stuart) writes that apart from a week exploring gardens around Nice and over the Italian border, and a trip to Zermatt walking in the mountains, there isn't really anything to say. Locally she has been touring the villages playing the organ in the churches and finds there is a demand to play for weddings and funerals. I meet Sheila regularly for coffee and a chat as she lives locally.

Jennie Bland (May) We were extremely sorry to hear of the death of Jennie's husband in January, and send her our deepest sympathy.

Liz Blood (Plant) Very little news this year! My husband has been on chemo, and I have a torn tendon in my right shoulder, have now had the op, so am out of action in my right arm for the moment! Have not done any travelling but hope to in the coming year. Was very sorry to read about **Jennie Bland (May)**'s husband. Jennie and I started at Sedgwick together, seems a long time ago!

Heather Gorton (Harris) I am keeping fairly fit and seem to be busier now than I was before retirement! Still involved with Fairford life. I work three days a week in Fairford Church Parish Office and continue to run the church flowers, which I love. I spent a few days in Venice last autumn when **Tina Tier** was supposed to be joining me but she broke her shoulder. However I am hoping she will visit the UK this year. I see **Linda Morley** who is not far away. Otherwise not much else to report. Can't believe it is sixty years since we left Westonbirt – how time flies!

Sue Hicks (Harker) John and I have had a surprisingly busy year, and found ourselves visiting our daughter and family in the Irish Republic, spending a few glorious days in Rome and visiting our twin town of Chambourcy, near Paris, as well as hosting visitors from Chambourcy. We enjoyed a beautiful river cruise on the Danube in August, preceded by a long weekend in Budapest. We found some much-needed sun in Tenerife in January, and then decided we should spend more time at home!

We are slowly decluttering now, mainly papers, in between our other activities. I belong to several U3A groups: French conversation (which I run), theatre, book chat, garden group, singing for pleasure and walking. I am in the twinning association and belong to a church in Lutterworth. The house and garden keep me occupied in my spare time, if any.

Ann Hildred (Jenkins) Last year I was taking some horrid pills which made me feel really ill, so much so that when I was in Canada, the rest of the party felt they needed to help me on and off the minibus and keep me upright when walking. It annoyed me very much! However I was given a radio-active pill (just one) in March, and since then I have felt much better and I have even recovered a bit of form at Badminton.

In the autumn I went on a trip to Rhodes and Cos with an archaeological group and saw Hippocrates' plane tree (supposedly!), the asclepeion, and lots of other things from classical Greece in the glorious sun. Otherwise life continues as usual, exercising the dog, going for sociable walks with friends, gardening, badminton, and seeing my daughters and grandchildren. I am really very lucky.

Anne Mercer (Seear) We remain staycationers and continue enjoying country dancing weeks in Scarborough. Last November we stayed on in order to visit Castle Howard for the first time, gloriously decorated for Christmas, and to admire the added attraction of the house modelled in gingerbread. Amazing!

We added another dancing week in Arnside in June and have booked to go again this June, taking afternoons to visit local interesting properties and friends. We have even begun a U3A monthly folk dancing group here, which has grown from eight to potentially two dozen dancers. If it grows any more we shall have to find another venue!

U3A has had some memorable monthly talks on:- behind closed doors at Holloway prison; years as a Detective Inspector; fantastic Falkland flowers and Zimbabwe, the jewel of Africa. We've also enjoyed outings to the Cotswold Wildlife Park, the Open Museum in Chalfont St Giles and Batsford Arboretum with the digital photography group, and also a Birmingham canal cruise and the Severn Valley railway. Not so much art this year!

Sadly my elder brother John died in May on the eve of his seventy-seventh birthday party, and my niece's husband suddenly this January, but there have been happier fortieth and fiftieth wedding anniversary celebrations, notably one at University College, Oxford.

In September we took Susan to revisit Westonbirt and were delighted to join a house tour led by **Angela Potter (Tracy)** followed by a family Holy Communion service at Malmesbury Abbey.

At the beginning of November building began on our youngest daughter's and husband's home, extending the ground floor and adding three more bedrooms and a bathroom. It has been fairly chaotic with parents, two teenagers and two younger siblings trying to lead normal lives. They hope it will be completed by Easter. On her seventeenth birthday, our eldest granddaughter became the proud owner of a Fiat 500. Where do the years fly? Meanwhile her brother sits his GCSEs in the summer.

Finally, it's a sad fact that even here in leafy Buckingham there is the need for a food bank, and I have joined the team that provides this service to add to my other commitments.

Margaret Squires (Renshaw) No great news. We just plod on attempting to get as close as possible to completing the list of 1557 Marilyns (hills with a drop of 150 metres between them and the next one). At the time of writing, I have forty left to do, but will never manage the St Kilda sea stacks. We had a trip to St. Kilda last year, and I know I could NEVER have done them.

Catherine Whittingham (Norman Moses) I think I must start every year by saying I have no news, but sometimes at our age "dull" is not a bad thing. John and I are both alive, reasonably well and have survived another year without breaking anything or having any body parts replaced.

We are still the guardians of Kaela, our nearly-sixteen-year-old granddaughter, and we are muddling our way through parenting again. Luckily she is doing well at school and seems to be as well adjusted as her peers, which might not be saying very much! Her fashion sense is a constant source of amazement, most of her wardrobe is bought at consignment stores!

The other grandchildren who live in Banff, Alberta, are all well, we will be meeting them in Alaska this summer for a family holiday. John and I haven't travelled much this year. We had a quick winter break in Florida and a trip out to Vancouver Island in August. Kaela seems to travel more than us at the moment. She is hiking in the Grand Canyon in March and volunteering in Costa Rica this July. I am amazed at the opportunities for teenagers today.

That is about it, I keep busy in a too-large house, which we will sell when Kaela finishes high school. I volunteer at the local food bank and belong to a Canada-wide group of grandmothers who since 2007 have raised over twenty million dollars for African grandmothers raising their own orphaned grandchildren. We manage to have a lot fun doing it. Golf, gardening and bridge keep me otherwise busy.

Section 27 (1957)
Section Representative:
Angela Potter (Tracy)

2017 marks the sixtieth year since the members of Section 27 left Westonbirt. Despite an offer to arrange something, sadly I have had only two responses from my Section to revisit old haunts. It is a pity in some ways as the school has re-invented itself, and I think that many of us, who left in 1957, would be delighted to see the improvements and experience the happy atmosphere.

On a less cheery note I heard from **Alison Robinson (De Courcy-Ireland)** on 30th March that **Emily Bilmes (Rawlence)** had died after suffering from Parkinson's for many years. Her sister **Elizabeth Ells** told Alison that it was expected and a merciful relief, as Emily had had no quality of life for a long time.

Those of you who remember **Katie Clarke** will be sad to hear that she died in January. She was such a bubbly teenager, but although she went on to have a successful musical career in Switzerland, her life seems to have been a mixture of highs and lows.

Joan Allan (Blakeborough) While spending Christmas with family in Cheltenham, I went over for lunch with **Angela Potter (Tracy)** and her family at Westonbirt, and then for a walk with Angela around the grounds of the school. (The school was closed for the holidays at the time.) It was lovely to catch up with them and to meet some of Angela's family too.

Life in Spain continues to be very pleasant but, due to Brexit (no comment), I am applying for an Irish passport, courtesy of my Irish grandmother! All currently goes well with the family and with us, apart from having to put down our beloved golden retriever. He came to us aged five, to walk Douglas. He was nearly fourteen and had done a great job. After a gap of about four months, Douglas now walks himself.

I still golf and we both play bridge. We held our annual family holiday, very successfully, at the end of July, this time at Drimnin, Morven, with all sixteen present.

No exciting foreign trips in the last year, but in August we spent five days in Orkney with friends. We drove up by car and crossed from Scrabster to Stromness, a ferry journey of ninety minutes, passing the Old Man of Hoy en route.

We found the islands enchanting, and so interesting due to the ongoing archeological discoveries (excavations of sites five thousand years old), and also the more recent history of the World Wars. The ground is so fertile and the climate amazingly temperate, quite different from Shetland. We wished we could have stayed longer.

Also in August, en route to visit my sister, **Helen Lilley**, near Newcastle, I had lunch with **Alison Reed (Hill)** and her husband, Anthony, at their lovely flat in Belford Hall, near Berwick.

Priscilla Boddington (Pentreath) A few days staying with **Gillie Drake (Strain)** in Guernsey was very enjoyable. We have a new rector in our parish, and it came out in a conversation with her last week that she had been taught by Gillie, in Kent, before Gillie was married! I have recently met **Barbara Anderson** for lunch in Salisbury when I was en route to my son in Hampshire.

At long last I am going to hand over as group leader of our local NADFAS church recording team, although I shall continue to record. It has been a fascinating activity since retirement.

News of my family's many and various activities keeps me entertained, and I look forward to seeing them as often as possible. With seven grandchildren between the ages of eight and twenty-six, there is plenty of their news, ranging from school plays to hockey, university life, European travel, journalism, marketing work, *et al.*

Judith Briggs (Walker) Last year started with a visit from my sister, **Annie (Ann Wingate)**, to us while in Cape Town which meant we visited the wine farms in Franschhoek and nearer in Constantia, Cape Town - great fun and good food and wine.

Later in the year we visited daughter, Alexandra, and her family in the US. They live just outside Boston, so an August visit there means hot weather, but good catch-up time with them all. The grandchildren are now fifteen (Claire at High School) and thirteen (Max and Charlie at Junior High). We hope that they will come and visit us at the Cape for Christmas this year so are planning accordingly and won't go over there.

Son, Guy, lives in Cape Town with his family (Anna, eleven, and Oliver, eight) so we see rather more of them.

We have just had a most interesting trip to Egypt. We joined a tour group at the end of January and spent the best part of two weeks there. All very hard work, but absolutely fascinating. Several days in Cairo, and then to Luxor and on a Nile boat for four days to Aswan.

Such amazing sights, temples and tombs, river and desert, so rich in history covering an immense span of time. Still trying to digest it all. No plans for further such excursions for the time being, but will head to the Cape for Easter and then to the game reserve area a little later on. We are still busy and involved and keeping going.

Christabel Cumberlege (Jaques) Thankfully, still in Somerset, the same house and garden. Not very computer literate, but looking forward to concerts and plant sales in the coming months, a family trip to Cornwall, and a visit to our elder son and his wife near Aberdeen, where they have returned to after seven years in Azerbaijan. Meantime, I am getting very excited about getting to Andalucia for a week's painting in May.

Vanessa Evans (Llewelyn) I send my love to all leavers of Westonbirt 1957. I live a busy life, still work three half days a week, at my orthoptic job for which I still have great passion. I teach recorder music lessons to three adults individually at my house, do yoga twice a week, swim once a week at the local YMCA, sing in a large choir of a hundred people one evening a week, walk every night about two miles with my husband, and still keep in contact with about five of my old Westonbirt friends.

Rowena Ginns (Cullin) On the 7th August, members of the Coaching Club drove from Badminton House to Westonbirt where we enjoyed a delicious lunch in the superbly restored library. Eight coaches and their teams of horses were an impressive sight on Piccadilly. The warm welcome was much appreciated, and the club members really enjoyed looking around the house and gardens.

We are in the process of renovating a flat in London to use as a meeting point for our far-flung family - long distance is quite a challenge! James is still based in Hong Kong, two grandsons there and two at university and school here. Jonathan is in the New Forest with the three younger grandsons, but travels all over the world as an in-house lawyer with INEOS. Bill has resigned as president of the Coaching Club, but we shall still enjoy our ten days at Royal Ascot and various shows.

Jenny Hayward (Williams) We may be away on 14th October. I have been in touch with **Ann Williamson**, **Ros Clarke (Langley)**, **Patricia Hegarty (Ballard)**, and **Penny Porter (Nicholson)**. It would be lovely to meet up with other old friends at WB. It would be nice to mark the occasion.

Not much news, except many trips to Cyprus during 2016 to organise bringing dogs Monty and Brownie to England. These were two large strays we had been looking after there, or rather paying someone to feed while we weren't there. They have both settled happily in UK. Monty is with son Tom in Bristol, and Brownie is here in Chipping Norton. We are now trying to civilize them! I went to Turkey and Rhodes with a friend on an organised trip in February but had to return early for the funeral of my eldest sister **Mary**, who had died in hospital after a short illness just before her 90th birthday.

Angela Potter (Tracy) My personal news, like many of my section, is not exciting. No big anniversaries, no new grandchildren – just increasing numbers of undergraduates! However I would like to tell you of my daughter-in-law's new book. *Patient H69: My Second Sight*. About four years ago she had a horrendous virus, which temporarily made her completely blind. The subject doesn't sound exciting, but believe me the book is difficult to put down. We continue to visit Prague fairly frequently as our daughter and her three children are there, and last summer we had a very jolly trip to Romania (amazing painted churches) with our local NADFAS, in fact we've recently had another, this time a guided tour of Palladian Villas in the Veneto. I recommend NADFAS as a holiday option – a good way to make new local friends too! I continue to guide unsuspecting visitors round the school 'state rooms', and **to that end have just completed another version of the history of 'Westonbirt House and the Holfords'. The astonishing thing,** which none of us wasted anytime over, all those years ago, is 'where did they get their money from?' I've searched this out exhaustively, and despite commonly held theories, really can't be sure. Occasionally, OGs turn up for these tours – last year I re-met Anne Sear (sorry don't know her married name). And very recently had three leavers of 1992 vintage.

Alison Reed (Hill) I have put October 14th in the diary in case you get interest in organising an anniversary event. Where have all the years gone?

I am afraid I have not got much to contribute this year. Anthony had a stroke six weeks ago, fortunately not as bad as I feared. He was in University College Hospital for five days. Since then we have had regular visits from speech therapist and physio, organised by the hospital's neurological department, and he is making progress. Fortunately, he can manage the stairs in our rather unsuitable house, and speech is gradually improving. But all quite time consuming.

Rhonnie Watts (Murray) My news is that I am fine. My family continues to grow, and I have eight grandchildren now. I haven't got back to tennis yet after breaking my ankle so badly, but hope to soon, and I am playing a lot of golf. I seem to keep very busy and spend quite a lot of my time caring for other oldies!

Ann Williamson I have had a limiting year. In 2016 my left hip became painful a few months after my right hip became satisfactory (after a new hip). When xrayed, I had to be admitted to hospital in November 2016. I still have many exercises until April. My idiopathic scoliosis was found to alter the organs in my body. I am being treated for those.

I am now beginning to get to some of the meetings of my groups. I could not play golf last year, but I hope to be able to play by July. I was unable to book holidays in 2016, so have booked to visit Sri Lanka in October. Unfortunately I will miss the Association Day. I still regularly see my nephews, their wives and children. I helped my nephews and nieces a great deal when they were young.

Section 26 (1956)
Section Representative:
Angela Potter (Tracy)

Sylvia Van Beek (Jackson) wrote to me last October to give the sad news that her sister **Ingrid Divett** (b.1942) had died after many years of illness. Poor Sylvia has had the depressing job and exhausting job of clearing out her flat.

I haven't had much of a response from Section 26 this year, but I'm not really surprised. Life is probably pretty full, but not necessarily of things that are newsworthy. That is certainly true for me, although I have managed to pad it out! My personal news is given under Section 27.

Jane Hancock (Quayle) We have just returned from a very enjoyable cruise, which went from Shanghai to Bangkok with calls in Japan, Xianen (China) Hong Kong, Vietnam and Cambodia. It was very cold at the beginning and very hot at the end (97F in Bangkok). We have also been on some other cruises this last year as we are working on the 'go now while we still can' principle! Fortunately we are both reasonably fit.

The main event of the year was our eldest granddaughter's wedding, which was in Cirencester on a fine and sunny day, and a lovely occasion. Our youngest granddaughter is now three. You may recall that two years ago she was diagnosed with a very malignant and rare brain tumour, so we are delighted that her latest scans have been clear. She seems fine mentally, but is still not walking unless holding on to someone or something. Hopefully this will progress with time.

Margaret Jackson (Grubb) I have no idea when I last sent news! I am still alive and not on any medication at seventy-eight, which others seem to find unusual. I don't do any formal exercise, just go for a short walk occasionally. I happily clerk Preston Quaker Meeting. I've done this for five years now, so next January there will be a change of clerk. Quakerism suits me very well indeed, after forty years as 'the Vicar's wife'! My husband Bob and I have just been on a two-week cruise to north Norway, hoping to see the Northern Lights. They didn't appear, but that's not going to ruin my life! My very absorbing hobby is beading: stitching tiny seed beads together to make jewellery, not stringing larger beads. I never seem to be in the vicinity of Westonbirt when there is anything going on, and it's quite a long way from Lancashire.

Cyrilla Potter (Monk) I have had a cyst on my good eye since November, and it has impaired my vision considerably. At present it seems to be diminishing in size, and I can see better. Writing has therefore been rather a challenge. A sight test has been refused until it goes. I had hoped to have temporary specs to tide me over.

We carry on here with increasingly younger new neighbours, which is rather jolly. Also we are lucky to have a lovely young carer/housekeeper and an extremely kind neighbour who shops for us and helps us in any way he can. I look forward hopefully to be able to see well enough to drive again.

Anne Renard (Matthews) The granddaughter of one of my best friends is to play a leading part in the triennial Greek play at Bradfield College. During my time at Westonbirt, I was fortunate to go to Bradfield twice – to *Antigone* and to *Oedipus at Colonus*. I had kept the programmes for both plays, and I have now passed them on to the current cast – quite a thrill. I shall always remember those occasions, as well as picnics at Chedworth and tea parties where we were treated to Hymettus honey, all organized by Miss Snow. She was a very inspirational teacher, interesting and interested, with a wide knowledge and love of the Classical world, especially of Greece. I was privileged to be taught by Miss Snow, and in my last term, by two more exceptional teachers. Miss Scott Smith, the new headmistress, and Canon Howard the new chaplain from St Peter's Hall, Oxford, were both Classicists.

Oriel Rogers Coltman (Corbett) We are still enjoying life in Shropshire, near to our children and grandchildren. They are all growing up fast – two at university, three about to do A Levels and then the anxious wait to see if they get the right grades. My garden is taking shape, and I am now having to restrain any mad ideas of extending it! We were at Westonbirt for the Gardens Illustrated Festival. Slightly disappointing because I picked the wrong talk, and the plants were not as good as I had hoped. We had a walk around the school garden. The anemones were wonderful, but the rest looked a bit unloved. When was the lake drained? I wonder if it was leaking or is for the dreaded Health and Safety? *(The lake had to be emptied to find out why it was leaking. The conclusion was that very expensive repairs are needed. If the conditions for the offered Lottery Grant can be met, these will be done. If not.... AP)*

Valerie Sill (Marsland) General domestic life, no excitement – boring news, but glad to be alive!

Section 25 (1955)
Section Representative:
Jill Gibson (Connor)

Thank you to those of you who responded to my request for news – it's good to keep in touch.

Elisabeth Abrahams telephoned to say she is looking forward to celebrating a significant birthday with her family in July by taking them to Aldeburgh, which is a favourite family place. She is still enjoying life, but at a bit slower pace with a few more restrictions than in her youth. Her grandchildren give her great joy. She attended the graduation of her elder granddaughter Joanna at Exeter last year. It was Elisabeth's birthday, and an early start to the day as the ceremony stated at 9am! Her younger granddaughter is in her first year at Bristol reading geography, and her grandson Simon is in his last year at school. She has been in contact with **Lynn Levy (Drapkin)** and through her sister **Madelaine** with **Pauline Davison (LeBrun)**.

Beth Barrington Haynes had a Christmas holiday in Budapest, where she enjoyed *La Bohème* on Christmas Day, performed in the Stata Opera House. She saw much of the greatly rebuilt city, took a Danube evening cruise and much more. Back at home, life is much as always with NADFAS and Opera Holland Park activities, and she still enjoys the farmland she owns with her brother, though last year was an expensive one with new land drains having to be installed.

Janet Davies (Norman Moses) says they are busy with the house being decorated at the moment, but other than the chaos that causes hasn't had a newsworthy year. Her husband had to have an operation on his hand which precluded them doing anything very interesting. She was hoping to go to Serena Jones party for local Old Girls on 25th March.

Bridget Frost (Kell) Yet another move! I don't recommend two moves in one year to anyone. Some of my furniture is in store in Somerset and some in London. Meanwhile I am living with my daughter, Laura, and her family. The flat has looked like a bomb site for two months, but hopefully I shall be in after Easter and there will be more to do even then.

Otherwise all well with the family. More interesting news next year, I hope.

Jill Gibson (Connor) As usual we have a busy life being kept occupied with Church and village commitments – working was much easier! We manage to see quite a bit of the family. The grandchildren are all growing up – eldest grandson in second year reading physics at Bath; eldest granddaughter in last year at Monmouth gives me an excuse to visit Westonbirt to watch her playing lacrosse. Those days of running around brandishing a lacrosse stick seem a long time ago! The rest, between eight and fourteen, are all involved with usual school activities and keep us well entertained with their tales. I was sorry not to be able to attend Serena's lunch. Unfortunately we were away from home that day, but I am sure those who could go thoroughly enjoyed meeting up.

Veronica Graham Brown (Howarth) I am well although a bit arthritic! I love living in East Devon and enjoy the village life of Colaton Raleigh. I became a new member of the PCC last night.

My four children are all fine, and my ten grandchildren all lead busy lives. One of my granddaughters, Hetty, graduated from Goldsmiths University last summer with a first in history of art. Seventeen-year-old Florence gained a place, and is in her first year at, Italia Conti in Guildford. Megan, my eldest granddaughter, is a nurse at Great Ormond Street.

I am looking forward to three nights in Nice at the end of the month with Hilary and John, my eldest daughter and son in law. I stay with friends in Dorset quite frequently and am hoping to drive or take the train to Salisbury before long to visit **Cyrilla Potter** and Roy.

Patricia Hedges (Crowe) I have had arthritis for eighteen months, and every time the steroids are reduced it comes back. However, I lead a normal life and have been over to Nice twice and also to Italy to see Tony and the dog. He is between Rome and Naples.
    I have a wonderful life in Torquay. I have been so fortunate. I speak virtually fluent French now and passed the DALF C2 exam last December, which allows one to study at a French university - not that I am going to do this! And I have found a group of people here with the same standard of French as myself. We meet twice a week to speak in French and often do other activities like having coffee together, meals out, theatres etc. It has made a big difference to my life to have them.
    Kevin and co are coming here for a week once GCSE exams are over. That should be July/August. It will be great to see them.

Sue Kennedy My daughter, Clare, living in Toronto, with her partner and two children, came over in August. The weather was a great addition to a lovely time had by us all. Cousins met up for the first time for several years, and it was a wonderful time, even with one sad loss of my daughter's beloved godmother, and she and her family attended the funeral in Wales. They had planned to get together but she died very suddenly at the age of ninety.
    At the same time as they came over, my son and his wife moved to Orkney! He had taken redundancy from his firm with a good package and was able to anticipate the move they were going to make when he retired. He has always loved that area and went on holiday there with his children a lot. I am trying to plan a visit, but getting up there is a nightmare!
    Apart from that, I am trying, mainly in vain, to drop one or two responsibilities as I approach eighty. It's difficult, though. These mainly are with church and Mothers' Union. My Guiding is nothing but fun and minimal responsibility at this stage in my life. Guiding is thriving well in Scarborough and we just need new leaders. What's new?

Alison Maguire (Mason) The last year has been dominated by my husband Bob being really quite ill. Happily now he is much better and can walk with a stick, instead of me pushing him around in a wheelchair.

What with him and the new puppy, I have not been able to think of writing on historical, architectural matters. I am rather disappointed with myself. Also, my sister, **Julia**, has had a serious stroke, which has worried us all. I am in touch with **Alyn (Paisley)**, **Vicky (Culme-Seymour)**, **Puff Drew**, and **Claudette (Llewelyn)**.

Penelope Pytell (Crankshaw) Life is quiet, and whenever possible, I am outside, but winters are long up here. We just survived a huge windstorm that took out power, in our area, for many days, but I installed a generator, a few years back, so had heat and light, though no internet, phone, etc. but was warm and safe. And, then, we immediately got snowed in for two days. Amazing snowfall, and have just managed to get all my doors to outside open - the challenges of living solo and growing old!

Love hearing from my old friends, and appreciate all messages and sharing our lives. Keep me up to date with any address changes, and especially email changes, because I hate to lose contact with people I have been writing to for a very long time.

Son, Jonathan is VP at Sothebys in Manhattan, and see him rarely. Daughter Nick is nearer, still at Corning Inc, and gets up to me for quick overnights, every other month or so. We never stop talking. Her visits are wonderful to me.

Watched the disaster in London today, and felt so sad. I send my best to anyone who remembers me.

Section 24 (1954)
Section Representative:
Alison Robinson (De Courcy-Ireland)

Once again, I am grateful for a fantastic number of replies to my request for news – an eighty-per-cent response rate when we are all at, nearing or past eighty is a testament to the longevity of the friendships we formed all those years ago and to our own resilience.

Jennifer Andrews (Clair) is now (to her section representative's delight) on email, although limiting her address to a select few and not venturing far in her computer use – no online banking or shopping planned for now. Jenny's eightieth birthday celebrations started with a visit to the RSC's production of *A Midsummer Night's Dream*, bringing back memories of being a fairy in a school production and running barefoot through the trees down to the lake and realising that her love of trees, gardens and books developed from those days.

She and Barrie now live quietly in Cornwall counting their blessings. Jenny's eleven-year-old great-nephew has recently started boarding school – a very different experience in these days of mobile phones and frequent home visits.

Elizabeth Bennett (Anning) says that she is alive and enjoys being as active as she can be, but feels she is short on news. However she very much enjoyed reading Ysenda Maxtone Graham's *Terms and Conditions, Life in Girls' Boarding Schools 1939-1979* which some younger reviewers thought was one of the funniest books of the year. Elizabeth's verdict: "FUNNY?? We woz there!!!"

Carolyn Crosse (Gurnhill) has had a fairly good year, despite Simon's mobility problems. They get about as much as they can, if slowly, and enjoy concerts, films, and the wonderful live screenings of ballet and opera at their local cinema. Carolyn herself is fit and strong and, with a carer coming in twice a week, still able to get to NADFAS and U3A. Her family is very supportive, six grandchildren keep them up to date and stimulated, and friends keep them sociable. Carolyn has an eightieth birthday (and party!) coming up this summer, and is also hoping to see **Jane Hopkinson (Milner), Sue Mitchell (Munro-Faure)** and **Jean Peacock (Binnie)** in the autumn.

Elizabeth Ells (Rawlence) is still living in the house she and Chuck built in 1963 on the banks of the Ottawa River in Ontario. When she remarried, Tom moved in and is enchanted by the river. It has been a very long cold and snowy winter this year, but they look forward to spring and being able to canoe and even camp again. Certainly sounds – as she says – that she is still fit and well, despite the odd "senior moment" (*join the club – AR*), still enjoys travelling, and spent ten weeks in Australia last year. She has two daughters living nearby and she sees them and her grandchildren regularly. One of them, Dr Louise Ells, has been awarded an Ontario Arts Council Writers Works in Progress grant, which makes the family very proud. Sadly Elizabeth's sister **Emily** died in March this year after suffering for years with Parkinson's and her other sister **Mary** struggles bravely and cheerfully with MS.

Amelia Gardner (Langford) says they are grateful for good health and pleasant surroundings, having now lived in retirement in Pembrokeshire for eighteen years, in a house they first saw and fell in love with forty years ago, after they were expelled from Nigeria. Ian continues his work translating the Bible in to the Abuan language, much aided by modern technology in consulting with the revision committee in Nigeria. This stage is almost complete but there are still several others to go before it is finally ready for publication.

Anna Grange (Hetherington) agrees it is bonanza year for eightieth birthdays. It doesn't seem to slow us down however, as Anna herself is learning to play bridge, despite feeling that she has left it somewhat late!

Rosemary Kitson (Hines) and her husband moved three years ago back near where they had lived forty years ago, and they are now happily ensconced in a lovely warm house with plenty of old friends nearby and thirteen grandchildren whom they see quite often.

Janet Knight (Sykes) is one of many who feel they have no special news, but who it is good to hear from and know they are still around! Janet is waiting for eye and hip treatments, which boringly slow her down considerably at present. She is in touch with **Gillian Sandeman (Wright)** and wonders if anyone has news of **Anne Israel (Cutriss)**, as she has not heard from her for some years now.

Sheena Mackenzie went to Jamaica for her middle grandson's beach wedding, but really likes to stay at home these days as she is tired of travelling and "now with all this airport security, it's just too much of a hassle". So instead, Sheena has invested in a new computer, frustrating her cat who is no longer able to sit on the keyboard and make a mess of things! Later that day, **Fiona Gray (Inskip)**'s techy son was coming round to sort out the computer's teething problems. Sheena comments that it is a strange chance that they both ended up in Nova Scotia!

Valerie Moorby (Holmes Johnson) celebrated her eightieth birthday in considerable style, with a family holiday in Tuscany and a birthday lunch in London.

Fortified by rejuvenated knees, she much enjoyed a trip with **Mary Rusinow (Worthington)** from Mary's home in Northern Italy down to Vis, a tiny island off the Croatian coast. Valerie comments "we must have looked quite an intrepid pair trundling our suitcases along and ignoring as far as possible the limitations of our combined 160 years"!

Valerie is enjoying her retirement from the bookshop, even though there is still sorting out to be done, and is looking forward to a granddaughter's wedding in Helmsley and a visit to Simon in San Francisco in the spring.

Heather Owen (Grange) is also in her eightieth year and busy comparing notes with fellow club members. She has had a busy and enjoyable year with lots of visitors, made easier by living next door to a super village pub. Heather spent a lovely week in Portugal with Tim and **Ann Lewis (Tyson)**, enjoying the birds and wild flowers while they played golf. All her grandchildren flourish, passing their driving tests and studying subjects as varied as musicology, contemporary dance, theatre costume and IT. Heather is rounding up as many as possible for the Annual Reunion and is hoping this will include at least **Ann Lewis, Anna Grange, Bridget Frost (Kell)** and **Bridget Maslin (Coleman)**.

Alison Robinson (de Courcy-Ireland) As I reached eighty two years ago, I can assure the rest of my section that life goes on much as it always did, albeit with a bit of creaking and less acute hearing! For me, the sobering thought is the realization that all three of my children are now in their fifties and the grandchildren in their teens and twenties! I continue as a Samaritan (a mostly sitting down occupation!), and, as well as much family involvement and enjoyable visits from **Heather Owen** and **Gillian Sandeman** and her husband, we have made several cultural trips this year, the most memorable being a visit to Herculaneum, which even in a cloudburst was absolutely fascinating.

Mary Rusinow (Worthingon) celebrated her eightieth birthday with two parties – one with the locals in her Italian village and the other, on her daughter's birthday in July, with daughters and grandchildren from Laos and New York, cousins from South Africa and friends from Denmark, Japan and Florida – quite a party! Mary also writes appreciatively of the trip she and **Valerie Moorby (Holmes-Johnson)** made to Vis, which she had long wanted to visit but couldn't while it was a military base. Mary still hopes to get to Albania one day, but meanwhile was off to visit Myanmar, then on to Laos to see her daughter and family before going back to Florida and then home to Italy with her Sheltie Dougal.

Gillian Sandeman (Wright) is planning to spend longer in UK this year and may even get to the annual reunion. She and Sandy celebrate sixty years of marriage this year but they certainly don't seem to be slowing down. Gillian writes:

We are both in pretty good health and still enjoying exploring the world. In July last we were in the Prespa Lakes area of Macedonia, Greece and Albania with a small group of friends and wild life specialists – amazing birds, butterflies, flowers, food, scenery and some frankly challenging drives in four-wheel drive vehicles on 'roads' of large rocks.

We recently came home from Vietnam and Cambodia. That involved very long flights but was absolutely worth it. A journey of contrasts from big cities (Hanoi, Saigon, Phnom Penh) to tiny villages on the muddy shores of the Mekong Delta – part of the journey was on a cruise boat on the Tonle Sap and Mekong Rivers. Wealth and poverty. Angkor Wat and Angkor Thom were highlights. The aftermath of brutal wars, napalm, the killing fields were still obvious, and often very moving as we heard individual stories.

Sandy, at eighty-four, is still carrying out research on corals and still going to Jamaica in aid of this: not a lot of corals in Ontario. I'm involved with fundraising for Jamaican schools and with boards and committees closer to home.

Our second great-granddaughter spent many months with us in her first year, while she and our daughter, who's raising her, waited for the Canadian baby's long term UK visa. It was lovely being so close to a tiny child again and watching the amazing physical and intellectual growth that happens so fast in the early months and years.

Section 23 (1953)
Section Representative:
Elizabeth Noyce (Clarke)

Thank you to all those of you who have responded to my desperate request for news. I am very grateful as life has not been easy recently. I do desperately need someone to take the job of Section Rep over from me. Much as I love doing it, I feel unable to carry on reliably.

Valerie Bell (Duckworth) I think I know how you feel – I recently found out I am 81 and it shows! Cannot remember anyone's names even when they are just introduced to me - in one ear and rushes out the other it seems! I am supposed to be secretary of a very small Red Cross Branch here in Uki, and it is a struggle to do the minutes for our three or four meetings a year! Last meeting was 28th February and haven't done them yet! I'm sure we are not alone.

We are recovering from great floods in this area, bigger than the last big one, which was in 1954. Lots of houses in low-lying areas have lost all they had stored or were using at ground level. But, the good news is that all the locals pitched in to help those in strife - a good sign when you compare the international news, which is all doom and gloom.

I send my good wishes to Westonbirt in all its different areas of activity and wish anyone who remembers me good luck, health and happiness.

Jenny Botsford (JJ Reynolds) New York and Toronto were the fun Christmas destinations for me, my eldest son, Charles, daughter-in-law and three university-age grandchildren. We stayed the first night in the very funky Ace Hotel, just near the Empire State Building, which we zoomed up first thing the next morning before moving to a lovely house in East 92nd Street lent to us by friends. From there we did all the sights, walked our feet off in Central Park, MOMA and the Guggenheim, were extremely moved by Ground Zero, chased around to see Grand Central Station, Times Square and the ice skating at Rockefeller Center, and drank in some amazing bars discovered by the boys. On Christmas Day we were delighted by our trip on the free Staten Island Ferry followed by walking the High Line, the old elevated railway converted to a wonderful garden walkway before our Christmas Dinner at Soho House New York.

We loved Toronto too, went up the CNN Tower and visited the markets and shops, as well as taking a day out to drive to Niagara Falls.

I sold my house in Kensington a year ago and downsized to a lovely flat just down the road. Built in 1935 like me, the building is art deco. I have part of the original guests' dining room, and have the only flat with French windows into the pretty garden, with a wide area outside where they used to have tables for diners in the summer. With only two bedrooms, there has almost been hot bedding with family and friends staying!

My other son, Chris, and his wife come over to England from Hong Kong often. They have a flat here in London. Chris's London office is now above the library in Kensington Town Hall, which is very handy for visiting Mama! Two of their children are still at university here but the eldest two girls are working in Hong Kong.

My cousin **Diana Ford (Paxman)** is also downsizing, selling her house in Kew and moving nearer her daughter in Wadhurst so cousin **Carol Lindsay Smith (Paxman)** and I have been helping Diana to sort her possessions. I also see **Penny Mann (Spurrell)** and her husband and am in touch with **Laura Marks (Lister)** in Australia.

Bronwen Brindley (Hywel Evans) I think I'm under the wrong section umbrella as I came to Westonbirt as a (just) twelve-year-old in 1946. I live, surrounded by family, in the North Yorkshire countryside, still teaching music, with husband John, emeritus professor who is still doing research into the origins of life, and golden retriever. Life is good and I feel very fortunate.

Looking back at life at Westonbirt at that period, I realise what a very good school it was, under a very distant but very fair Head, Violet Grubb, and equally good and fair housemistress, Miss Lilley. I was, perhaps, fortunate in having good friends, but I never experienced or was aware of any bullying or repression. There were few frills. It was cold in winter and the food was awful, but we were used to that, having been through the war. There was a strong sense of loyalty to the school and to one's House, and we were encouraged to be concerned about one another. There was an entrance exam - I was a music scholar - and several Oxbridge candidates each year, and the school had a very good all-round reputation. There were about two hundred and fifty girls in all, about fifty in each of five Houses. Dorchester was, of course, the best!

Caroline Fuchs (Kell) I am still alive, but have no particular news!

Moira Gilbert (Melvin) Peter and I had a joint eightieth birthday celebration at the end of July, with all the family and many great friends. I still go birdwatching and visit historic houses, though having knee problems, I cannot walk too far now. We shall be making our regular trip to Scotland in June.

Deidre Gordon (Pinnington) I am alive, still working as a psychotherapist part-time, running house and land, plus two boisterous young bloodhounds. I enjoy driving my Aston Martin, when the weather is good, but also have to cope with a husband who is showing signs of slowing up and turning into a Mr Meldrew!

Deidre's advice: Keep smiling, even when the teeth are gritted and you are hanging on with your fingertips! (Thank you for that advice. Liz)

Anne Greenstreet (Selby) This growing old business is not a picnic!

We struggle on in Camberley. Luckily there are lots of local things to do, and Anthony (89) helps in the Heritage Gallery where we have both given short talks. I also enjoy U3A Art Forum once a fortnight and NADFAS every month. Thank goodness WB taught us to speak UP - so many people/speakers mumble.

We see our family as often as we can. Eldest granddaughter is in her second year at Manchester, and the second is off to Australia for a gap year. The other seven are still at school in the Twickenham area. Lizzie, with cystic fibrosis, has quite a struggle, but plays games, skis and trampolines - all good for the lungs. The various new drugs are slow to get approval, which is sad, as they would make so much difference.

Both our daughters are journalists. Rosanna has had her Guardian column for more 25 years!

Gillian Henson (Groome) Another year slips by, helping out with grandchildren, swimming, playing mahjong, arranging sites for the sketching club, and London exhibitions. Added to this, refreshing trips to Juan les Pins, Overy Staithe Norfolk, Seville and Cordoba.
New for me this year is Pilates, following a problem with walking any distance. I am now cured, thanks to these exercises. I keep active and busy, but only as busy as I want to be.

Sally Hollister (Boston) Sorry, I haven't communicated much over the past years but time gets away from me together with everyday problems. I myself am fine. Unfortunately my husband, Walt, has developed Alzheimer's, so I am taking care of him 24/7. I continue to teach my aerobic dance classes twice a week and sing in our church choir, so that keeps me connected to the outside world. I still keep in touch with some of my friends from Westonbirt and try to see them every time I come back to England. It's always a treat to get together with them whenever possible. As we all know, old friends are your best friends.

Rosemary Mulholland (Hawkins) We are having an exciting time at the moment as our younger son James is engaged to Harriet Stuart Menteth with a wedding in June in Scotland. So despite being only the parents of the groom, we seem to be busy organising travel, outfits and accommodation for the dog, the cat and us!
Anyway, we are busy and pretty well despite the odd bump. My bilateral arthroplastie continue to give me a new lease of life, thanks to a wonderful surgeon. John Charles lives on London and is working hard for a firm called Profit. After two A4 sides of job description, I was none the wiser. He has a Russian girlfriend whom we hope to meet at the wedding.

Elizabeth Noyce (Clarke) 2016 was not a good year as aging does not suit me! My main problem is mobility – or lack of it. I have had to give in and buy a "Wheelie"! (Beautiful purple!) After a long time refusing to acknowledge the need, I am now thankful that I can walk about a bit more, albeit slowly. Asthma and attendant breathing problems have also needed attention. At least I can still drive, so have a bit of independence. Enough of problems, let's get on with the news!

Sadly, we lost our beloved King Charles Spaniel last April. He was almost fifteen, so he'd had a good life, but we still miss him terribly. We have not been able to get another dog as our lack of mobility precludes daily walking, and it would not be fair to go without regular exercise.

We went to the Cantabrian area of Northern Spain for a holiday last June and loved it, an area we had not ventured before. We also did our regular trips to Cornwall in April and October, and to Normandy in November, though how much longer we shall be able to do that remains to be seen. I remain a member of the U3A and attend regular meetings and go on outings to places of interest. I also still attend the twice-a-term lunches of the Oxford Women's Luncheon Club, where we have some interesting speakers, and the local WI is still on the programme.

Some of you will remember our sister Katie; she led a very varied life causing many problems, and some successes throughout her life, one success being a regular member of the cast for several years at the Bayreuth Festival. She spent most of her latter years living on the French/Swiss border. No-one really knows what she did with herself in those years. The shock came when the police informed me in November that she was on a ventilator in intensive care in King's College Hospital in London. Apparently she had been living in London for some time. My name was the only contact that they could find amongst her possessions. I had to contact her son, who was naturally shocked and a bit puzzled as to how she had got to where she was. She was eventually taken off the ventilator and sadly died on the 9th December.

Where does the time go?! My family have all virtually grown up now! Natalie (23) graduated from Southampton last summer and has spent the winter as a chalet girl in the Alps. Her brother Matthew (20) is doing an apprenticeship with a subsidiary (I think!) of Network Rail. At present it seems to be that he gives advice on computer problems. Alex (21) graduates this summer from Birmingham, and Victoria (18) does her A Levels this summer. She plans to have a year out before going to uni at Nottingham next year.

Time to stop now! I do hope that a kind person will come forward to continue with Section 23's news. I shall miss doing it myself, but feel that, due to increasing health difficulties, I am no longer able to time myself to do the job properly. I hope that you all have a good year without too many problems arising from that part of life called "Elderly"! (I don't like the word "Old"!) Good Luck to all my friends! Liz ("Bubbles")

Section 21 & 22 (1951 & 1952)
Section Representative:
Margot Gill (Wilcox)

Elizabeth Daly I visited the Windsor Horse Show in 2016 which was put on for the Queen's ninetieth birthday. It was amazing. I spent a week in Salcombe, Devon, when they were remembering the terrible lifeboat tragedy during the Second World War. I found it a very enjoyable place with excellent shops and good food facilities. **Kirsten Birchenough (Krabbe)** now lives in Wimborne, and **Jennifer d'Oley (Jennings,)** lives in Devon so I have lost my links. I do see my sister **Sarah Wallington (Daly)** who lives quite close.

Margot Gill (Wilcox) Many thanks to those of you who sent news, it is much appreciated. Last year I had a fortnight driving up the A1 stopping in Stamford for three days with a ninety-three-year-old Shell colleague, across the Pennines and on to Bridge of Allan for another three days, then down the M6, M5 to Worcester all in very heavy rain. I was so looking forward to the views across the Pennines, but no such luck.

A river boat from Lyon to Avignon was a very relaxing week, wine-tasting and enjoying the wonderful views.

For the first time in years I spent Christmas away, with three weeks in Denver with friends, and it didn't snow. Home life is kept very busy with Shell Pensioners and of course the Church. The Ringwood community centre has some very interesting lecture series with excellent speakers. This spring there are some good ones on English poets. May you all have a healthy and happy year.

Susan Kavanagh (Harris) This year has been my most active and unexpected since my husband passed away some fifteen years ago. March to April I was in Germany with daughter Celia and family – spent a few days visiting Bruges and Ostend – then a week in the UK visiting family. I also stayed with **Jane Sutton** for a couple of nights.

The unexpected was that on my return to California, I "knew" that I must sell my mobile home where I have been extremely happy these past twelve years and return to my old home to live with my son. This is only for the time being as the plan is that later this year I hope to return to the UK to live, while keeping my official base here.

During the summer my two beloved granddaughters were over from Germany for a month, revisiting family and friends, followed by Celia coming over to help me move back to our old home (which we bought years ago). And here I am enjoying the wettest winter in several years, truly a Godsend as the drought here was extremely severe – and with plenty of sunshine too.

Finally I'd like to add that I have seen **Mary Hall (Sercombe)** and family many times, she became a great-great-grandmother late last year. This week I became a great-great aunt for the first time! There is much still to enjoy at my age."

Jane Palmer (Needham) writes that she is lucky to have her family living nearby. Since her husband, David, died five years ago, they have kept her busy. She loves her garden (using kneelers these days) and enjoys painting classes, NADFAS talks and supporting charity events. Jane had a lucky escape last year when the barn she lives in caught fire. Thanks to her son's Rhodesian Ridgeback who barked and barked until his family (Jane's son and family who live in her original manor farm house) woke up and rescued Jane. Luckily the fire brigade were wonderful.

Granddaughter Annabel went to Harper Adams and gained a first in business management and marketing, and then took three months off to tour the USA and stayed with **Daphne H**.

Ann Sadler (Millard) endeavours to keep active and plays table tennis three times a week. Mercifully she is not a committee member of the WI after nineteen years as secretary and four years as president. After seventeen years, she is still the secretary of the PCC because no-one else will take it on (*join the club Ann, M*) and is treasurer of the bellringing group, but has not been able to ring for a while as she has had a shoulder replacement. Her widowed daughter is living with her while her old (1600's) house is being renovated. Her youngest grandchild is still living with her – twenty and at college.

Jennifer Springett says that there is nothing to report – very boring.

Jane Sutton I am grateful for good health which has enabled me to keep busy here and also get overseas a lot.

Sadly there is a lot being said about older people being lonely, and I am grateful that that is not something I suffer from. My front door opens onto the towpath of the Kennet and Avon Canal. So many people walk past my flat, often with their dogs. Fishermen sit and fish. Many species of waterfowl float by, and narrow boats often moor up for the night alongside the path.

I am now the chair of three committees, which include our local Christian bookshop (Shoemakers), Newbury YMCA and our Christians Together in the Newbury areas (CTNA). Taking services in some village churches also keeps me in contact with many folk.

I did something I never thought that I would do, and that was going on a coach trip through twelve countries and along the Adriatic coast in May. It was so beautiful and interesting. I also paid a weekend visit to Ireland as it was the easiest way to get to the Isle of Man to see an old friend there. I returned from two weeks in Cuba at the beginning of February, travelling 1,600 miles from one end of the island to the other. Just in time – Cuba is beginning to be flooded with tourists, especially from Canada. I fulfilled two dreams: to drink coconut milk from a coconut and to swim with a dolphin.

Section 19 & 20 (1949-50)
Section Representative:
Serena Jones

Sarah Abel (Poynor) Not much has changed since last year, except that my failing memory has slowed me down. I am still looking after myself unaided and have managed to have several days out, thanks to my senior rail pass. I spent Christmas cruising on the Oriana, which I enjoyed very much, and have frequent visits from my sons and their families, which keep me busy.

Meriel Pickett (Sharpe) I've had a lovely year in the garden, greatly improved by coppicing the shelter belt of sweet chestnut, untouched for at least sixty years! You can imagine the light let in, and a carpet of wild violets and primroses appeared, followed by cowslips in many colours.

In October I went to the Hague and Delft on a short NADFAS trip to look at glorious pictures. It made me realise that I can no longer keep up with sprightly sixty-year-olds, so I shall have to repeat river cruising adventures.

I went to Vansad in the spring, and was delighted to welcome my Hungarian granddaughter on her first flight alone in July. She is now at a school supported by the German government, where all lessons are taught in German – three languages so far, and hoping to begin Spanish.

Jo Smith (Pick) Still in North Norfolk. Bridge, golf, gardening and lovely beach walks. Went to Italy for Christmas to stay with family.

Beryl Thorp (Holm): The problem with getting old is that one gets a bit slower and is surprised to get tired and exhausted. I am fortunate I can still drive and get about quite well. I belong to the U3A, which has so much to offer, with interesting talks as well as a world of music, with some excellent concerts both locally and in Birmingham. I enjoy the theatre and try to support our local group, as well as going to some of the excellent productions in Malvern. Some of these go on to London.

After a lapse of over forty years, I have started tower bellringing again and have started handbell ringing too. We give little concerts in residential homes and to the local dementia centre.

I have a wonderful ninety-three-year old friend who has more energy than me and says we must "think positive"! We have just returned from a lovely holiday in Gran Canaria and are now planning next year's holiday.

Elisabeth Wells (Burt) April saw me in Berlin for the civil marriage of my grandson Tom to Katha, lovely sunny weather and we were able to be in the garden looking its best, thanks to my daughter, Alona's efforts.

Lucy returned to the City after twelve years and is happy working away as if she had never left. Whatever you may have read, it really can be done. Caspar took and passed the JIEB, and I went to his graduation in June at the Chartered Accountants Hall, an interesting venue.

In July we had a family wedding in Sussex, a splendid venue with plenty of space for young relatives to rush about in safety without tripping up the older guests. Early September saw me in Schloss Ehreshoven, just outside Cologne, for Katha and Tom's truly magnificent church ceremony. (The German system is to have this well after the official marriage.) The English family turned out in force. We had three days of celebrations followed by a dreadful journey home, with heavy rain travelling with us. Now I look forward to my eighty-fifth birthday next month with overseas family flying in.

Elizabeth Wicks (Butcher) Life is still great and plenty of interesting things to do. I went with my elder daughter and husband for three wonderful days in June to Barcelona and in October for a few days with friends to Sicily. I feel very lucky to still be sound in mind and limb. I see **Jennie Deane (Mills)** and **Anne Matthews**, the former living nearby in Wye.

Sections 17 and 18 (1947-48)
Section Representative:
Pauline Jackson (Garrett)

Jennifer Barton says "Who was it who painted a sun on the reproduction of a Paul Nash landscape hanging in the Parlour? It wasn't me, but I was reminded of watching whoever it might have been when visiting the Nash exhibition at Tate Britain." Jennifer enjoyed seeing this and other exhibitions in company with **Helen James (Bashall)**, which brightened up the icy cold days in February. She was glad of a warmer weekend soon afterwards when tackling Selsey garden's invasive wild garlic in a few short bursts of energy before relaxing while watching another exciting Six Nations rugby match. Overall, Jennifer finds herself fortunate in having had a pretty similar twelve months to last year.

Primrose Minney informs us that she now lives in the grounds of Lawford House, which has been bought by a developer, who is going to put up eight posh houses in the paddock area. Primrose does not mind this, as some builders want to build hundreds of houses! Lawford village already has five thousand residents.

Hilary Nicholson (Bishop) continues with the Arts Society and Church Recorders and U3A and recently enjoyed a holiday with her family in Devon. Hilary's eldest grandson is getting married next summer and will be continuing with training with Youth With A Mission in Brisbane.

Section 16 (1946)
Section Representative:
Jane Reid (Bottomley)

Acknowledgements of the AGM 2016 notice and of the 2017 Spring Newsletter were received from **Patricia Krichauff (Faulkner)**.

Sylvia Landsberg described herself as "one of the oldies, though no grand or great-grandchildren. As a garden historian and as a wartime Westonbirt pupil, looking back I still marvel at our luck then in having lived at Bowood, Corsham and Westonbirt and their glorious grounds.
   "Gardening is still my preferred activity. Too late to plant an arboretum, was my thought twenty years ago, but now too late for a shrubbery or even herbaceous border to reach fruition. So annuals it will have to be, perhaps one tree for posterity!"

Elizabeth Watson (Allen) sent her news promptly as she was about to have an operation on her spine and would be otherwise engaged for some time! She wrote that she found that as one got older, one did less, and rather slowly, but she still seemed to be pretty busy. She entertained quite frequently even if only six at a time, was always painting to keep up with exhibitions, and helping other OAPs. She enjoyed NADFAS and all the trips that were arranged. They went to northern Spain last June and to Lincoln in September.
   Elizabeth is in touch with **Jean Speirs (Norman)**.

Section 15 (1945)
Section Representative:
Serena Jones

June Fulford (Layborn) Absolutely no news! Widowed for nigh on eighteen years. Approaching 89 myself (I think Westonbirt and I are the same age). Still standing, with three and a bit great-grandchildren, who are a joy, but have lost too many of my contemporaries locally, my holiday and cinema friends, all very sad. Still in touch with **Liz Hosegood (Robertson)** and **Pauline Cooper (Nock)**.

Mercia MacDermott (Adshead) As I shall be celebrating my ninetieth birthday in 2017, my activities are becoming more limited, but I still attend a weekly group that meets to practice French conversation, and I am still President of the Friends of Worthing Museum.

A major recent event in my life was the publication by Manifesto Press of my latest, and probably last, book: *Once Upon a Time in Bulgaria*, a country with which I have been closely associated since 1948 and where I lived and worked for some sixteen years as a teacher in a secondary school and, later, as a university lecturer prior to 1989. Aimed at the general reader, especially anyone planning to visit the country, my book combines essential information about the history, culture, customs and traditions of Bulgaria, with some of my own memoirs of my life there, including my extraordinary experiences as a celebrity after my biography of Bulgaria's most beloved national hero, intended to inform British readers, was translated into Bulgarian and unexpectedly became and remained a bestseller in Bulgaria itself.

Constance Ware phoned me just after last year's News was printed to apologise for missing it and to say that her year had been dominated by a broken shoulder. She had been out to see a particularly high tide and slipped over on mud. She confirmed that she was recovering well.

Sections 13-14 (1943-44)
Section Representative:
Jean Marr

Felicity Atkinson (Fizzy Sutton) Fizzy is delighted to have found that she has not got Parkinson's but her mobility is not as good as it was. She celebrated her ninetieth birthday last October with a party of over one hundred friends and family.

Gillian Blum (Gregory) I have no interesting news. I am well. I celebrate my ninety-first birthday in February with family and plan to keep going for another few years.

Rosemary Campbell (Fraser) My main news is that I was ninety in October 2016 and had a huge tea party in the primary school here in Aldermaston where I had been governor for thirty-two years (1958-1990). A very happy occasion, with some cousins, and lots of friends from the village and elsewhere. My three children spoke of my life and there were photos of my past, some reminiscences of people I still work a little with. A frame and a stick, plus a friend's arm, get me regularly to church where we have a wonderful rector, daughter of David Winter who writes marvellous books. She visits me regularly in spite of having six parishes, so I am very lucky.

Mary Capey (Reynolds) has had problems with her hip and has had operations, and I am pleased to record successful. Her plan now is to move to a sheltered flat. She plans to continue singing in the choir, and she is looking forward to resuming her crafts.

Patricia Hall (Dickinson) The highlight of 2016 was my ninetieth birthday in July. My daughters had booked a holiday in Coverack in Cornwall, a lovely house that sleeps ten, so at different times my three grandsons and their partners came to stay. Later in July they arranged a garden lunch party for over fifty friends and relatives, luckily the weather was very kind to us.

Jean Marr I quite agree with Susan Yealland (see below). I feel very much the same. I am trying to help so many people with problems. First I want to thank you all for writing with your news. I am going to send all this from Sections 13-14 to **Debbie Young**, the news editor, and hope she can read my writing. *(Ed: I hope I got it all right!)* I want to thank **Jane Reid** for all the help she has given me over the past years. I am still standing up but not able to walk very far, but am grateful for a wonderful taxi service.

I am busy with my church which is active and friendly. I try and do Sudoku puzzles daily to keep my mind active and walk as much as I can. I think it is important to talk to people every day. I am very sorry for people on their own. I will be ninety this October.

Yvonne Phillips (McIlroy) I am still in the same house and still enjoying it and my garden. I am active and able to drive, play bridge, and see a lot of my marvellous family. Ninety is not all that bad.

Susan Yealland (Simpson) had "absolutely no news at all". She wrote that she was just ambling along, still arthritic but ok in the head, the sadness is in losing so many friends and acquaintances or sinking into dementia and unable to have a good conversation with them - and wondering what will happen to oneself.

Sections 1-12 (1931-42)
Serena Jones (Sections 1-8), Pauline Jackson (Section 9), Rebecca Williams (Sections 10-12)

No news returned this year.

And finally... are you decluttering?

To those of you who have made it to this page, and who may be having a clear-out due to downsizing or moving house, here is a plea for you to donate any unwanted old copies of the News, or any school memorabilia, for the archives.

Please send any donations to Mrs Bridget Bomford, Archivist, at the School. If in doubt, please phone her first on 01666 880333, to check that what you are offering would be welcomed.

Invitation to Westonbirt Association Members

Westonbirt School always welcomes alumnae, whether on formal occasions such as Association Days, or for informal visits to reminisce about your school days. There's always something new to see, in terms of academic and extra-curricular activities, new buildings and projects to restore the old, and current pupils are always fascinated to meet their predecessors. You are also very welcome to bring your family, even if you have no daughters or granddaughters to follow in your academic footsteps!

In the interests of security, and to make sure we are able to welcome you on your preferred date, please contact Miss Alison Salih, PA to the Headmistress, to arrange your visit by calling 01666 880333 or emailing asalih@westonbirt.org.

Whether or not you plan to visit the school in person, you may also like to visit our website, which is constantly being updated with school news and photos, as well as a picture gallery from the archives.

How to Contact the Westonbirt Association

The Westonbirt Association database is kindly managed by the School, and so the School is now your first point of contact for any enquiries regarding the Association. Miss Alison Salih, PA to the Headmistress, will be able to direct you to the most appropriate person, according to the nature of your query. She will also be able to provide contact details for your Section Representative, whose personal information is no longer included in the News Magazine for the sake of their privacy.

Incidentally, please don't forget to let Alison know if your own contact details change, so that we can keep you informed of Association matters and can find you if any of your former classmates are looking for you. If you're a fan of social media, you may also enjoy networking with us on the alumni Facebook page:

www.facebook.com/groups/108986984329/

Alison works at the school full time, year round, so is generally available during office hours. You may reach her via the main school telephone number, 01666 880333, or by emailing her at asalih@westonbirt.org. She is always glad to hear from past pupils.

How to Order Copies of the Westonbirt Association News

Since 2015, to gain efficiencies, save costs, and to take advantage of advances in modern technology, we have changed the way we produce and distribute the Westonbirt Association News.

If you are a regular subscriber, you are welcome to go on receiving your copy as before, despatched by the News Finances and Distribution Officer, Jenny Webb, for as long as your account with her is in sufficient credit.

However, you will also now be able to order the latest edition, and all future editions, online, wherever you live in the world. Your copy will be printed in your local territory and sent at local postage rate. If you do this while your account with Jenny is still in credit, she will refund the balance on request - or if you prefer, you may simply donate the balance to the Westonbirt Association Memorial Bursary Fund.

If you prefer not to order online, you may also be able to order a print copy from your local high street bookshop by providing them with the ISBN number of the latest edition. (For the 2016 edition, the ISBN is 978-1-911223-06-1.)

If, on the other hand, you are one of the many people who prefer these days to read ebooks, you may prefer to order an ebook version, which will be made available via all the mainstream ebook platforms, including Kindle, Kobo and iBooks.

We are confident that this is the best way forward for the long-term interests of the Association, and we hope it will also appeal to the younger generation (and many of the older ones!) who enjoy using digital technology. Please be assured, however, that we will always produce print copies for those who prefer them, and also for our substantial Association News archive.

Westonbirt Association
Memorial Bursary Fund

The Westonbirt Association Memorial Bursary was set up in the late 1940s in memory of the five former Westonbirt pupils who lost their lives during the Second World War while they were members of the Forces, Civil Defence or the Nursing Services.

The aim of the fund is to give a bursary each year to help fund the school fees of girls at the school. The Memorial Bursary is still running today, and each year the Association makes an award from this fund to help towards the sixth form fees of one or more pupils.

To be considered for the Memorial Bursary, girls must be nominated by the school in the spring of their Year 11. Candidates complete an application form and are interviewed by a panel from the Westonbirt Association Committee. The process provides good experience for later job and university applications, and, for the successful candidate, receipt of the award enhances their CV as well as providing welcome financial help. Once awarded, payment is made for both years of the recipient's Sixth Form.

Over the years, we have helped more than eighty pupils in this way. With income levels from investments so low at present, and school fees rising, new donations are always welcome to increase the value of the award.

How to Donate to the Memorial Bursary Fund

Cash donations

Payments may be made by cheque payable to "Westonbirt School" and should be clearly marked for the Westonbirt Association Memorial Bursary Fund.

Online by standing order

Please reference payment in the following format:

> Account name: Westonbirt School
> Sort code: 200384
> Account number: 30951927
> Bank: Barclays

Bequests

As the school is a charity, bequests are free from liability to inheritance tax. The following are suitable words to send to your solicitor with a request that the Westonbirt Assocation Memorial Bursary be included in your will:

> *"I bequeath to Westonbirt School in the county of Gloucestershire the sum of £x, free of duty, to be used for the purposes of the Westonbirt Association Memorial Bursary."*

You might also wish to inform the school as follows:

> *"I intend to make a bequest to the school for the purposes of the Westonbirt Association Memorial Bursary."*

GiftAid Declaration for the Westonbirt Association Memorial Bursary

If you are a UK taxpayer, the school can reclaim tax on any gifts you make, via the Gift Aid scheme, provided you fill in the declaration form below in full and return it with your first gift.

Please treat as Gift Aid donations all qualifying gifts of money made *(please circle as applicable)*: today / in the past 4 years / in the future

I enclose a donation of £.......... as a contribution to the Westonbirt Association Memorial Bursary.

I confirm I have paid or will pay an amount of income tax or capital gains tax for each tax year (6 April to 5 April) that is at least equal to the amount of tax that Westonbirt School and all other charities that I donate to will reclaim on my gifts for that tax year. I understand that other taxes such as VAT and council tax do not qualify. I understand the charity will reclaim 25p on every £1 that I give on or after 6 April 2008.

Title_____ Forename _____

Surname _____

Address _____

Postcode _____

Signature _____

Date _____

Please notify Westonbirt School if you want to cancel this declaration OR change your name or home address OR no longer pay sufficient tax on your income and/or capital gains. If you pay income tax at the higher or additional tax rate and want to receive the additional tax relief due to you, you must include all your Gift Aid donations on your self-assessment tax return.

Please send donations and the completed form to:
The Finance Manager, The Bursary, Westonbirt School
Tetbury, Gloucestershire GL8 8QG
Registered Charity Number 311715

*We would like to thank Alanbrookes Ltd
for kindly auditing the Association's accounts.*

ALANBROOKES LTD
CHARTERED ACCCOUNTAND AND REGISTERED AUDITOR

We aim to bring transformational change to local businesses
and the lives of their owners.
Please call Andrew Fisher for a free exploratory meeting
on 01453 889559 or email andrewfisher@alanbrookes.co.uk
www.alanbrookes.co.uk

www.ingramcontent.com/pod-product-compliance
Lightning Source LLC
Chambersburg PA
CBHW071347080526
44587CB00017B/3008